UNITED STATES MINT

2019 ANNUAL REPORT

parkerpub.co

Published by Parker Publishing Company

www.parkerpub.co

David J. Ryder
Director
United States Mint

DIRECTOR'S LETTER

It is my privilege to present the 2019 Annual Report of the United States Mint. During Fiscal Year 2019, the Mint successfully executed its mission by:

- facilitating commerce by providing trusted and secure United States circulating coinage to meet monthly orders from Federal Reserve Banks (FRBs);

- minting and issuing precious metal bullion coins (gold, silver, platinum, and palladium);

- minting and issuing other national coins and medals (proof and uncirculated versions of circulating coins, commemorative coins, and other coins and medals); and,

- serving as the Department of the Treasury custodian for the Nation's gold and silver reserves.

During FY 2019, the Mint shipped more than 12 billion circulating coins, and completed our fifth consecutive year of 100% on-time delivery of circulating coinage to FRB locations. The Mint also produced 18.8 million ounces of bullion during FY 2019, as well as 4.3 million units of numismatic products.

I am especially proud of the manner in which the Mint improved the financial performance of its numismatic program. During FY 2019, the Mint's numismatic program generated $349.6 million in revenue and $1.7 million in net earnings. This represents an improvement of 19.3% for revenue and 111.1% for earnings over the previous year. These impressive results were a key reason the Mint was able to transfer $540 million to the Treasury General Fund at the end of FY 2019.

One of my primary goals as Director of the Mint has been to establish successful joint numismatic products with foreign mints. It has been my vision to coordinate with mints from different nations to offer unique products that are equally popular in the United States and abroad. I was very pleased to see this vision become a reality during 2019, as the United States Mint successfully launched joint products with both the Royal Australian Mint and the Royal Mint of Spain involving our Apollo 11 50th Anniversary Commemorative Coin program. In July, it was my honor to help launch the *Pride of Two Nations* coin set, developed in collaboration with the Royal Canadian Mint. The response to each of these joint products has been overwhelmingly positive.

Thinking creatively and operating "outside the box" were essential to the United States Mint's ability to successfully produce and market two well-received commemorative coin programs in 2019: The Apollo 11 50th Anniversary Commemorative Coin program and the American Legion 100th Anniversary Commemorative Coin program. The Apollo 11 program included a 3-inch, 5-ounce, curved coin – the first time the Mint has produced a curved coin at this size.

I am very proud of the Mint's production, sales, and delivery accomplishments during FY 2019. However, the achievement in which I have the greatest amount of pride is in the area of employee safety. The Mint's Total Recordable Case Rate (TRCR) for safety incidents during FY 2019 was just 1.45. This is the Mint's lowest TRCR since we began collecting and tracking this data. By comparison, the TRCR for comparable private sector manufacturing operations was 4.9, more than three times the rate of the Mint.

I believe that a key to the Mint's success is the fact that we take the safety of our staff very seriously, and our staff know that we do. Full-time safety staff in each Mint facility coordinate closely with the Environment, Safety, and Health leadership at Mint headquarters to ensure we take every reasonable precaution to prevent accidents where anyone can get hurt. Achieving the type of safety record realized by the Mint only happens when safety is part of an agency's culture. I am very impressed by how Mint staff take ownership for safety through every step of our manufacturing process.

I was very pleased with the enthusiastic public response to the Mint's introduction of both pennies and quarter dollars with a "W" mintmark, indicating the coins were produced at the West Point Mint. The "W" penny and "W" quarter-dollar both generated significant renewed interest in our circulating coinage. I am eager to build on that enthusiasm by working with Congress to establish new circulating coin programs to run starting in 2022. The Mint has conducted extensive market research to identify the types of circulating coin programs that would resonate most strongly with the American public. It is my hope that Congress will enact legislation for new circulating coin programs that is consistent with the Mint's recommendations.

This year the Mint increased its focus on anti-counterfeit efforts, in support of both our bullion and circulating coin programs. The United States Mint's reputation for the purity and weight accuracy of its bullion coins is unquestioned. To ensure the continued integrity of the Mint's bullion program, Secretary of the Treasury Steven T. Mnuchin recently approved the Mint to move forward with steps to enhance the security of our bullion products. I am confident the new measures we implement will significantly enhance the security of the Mint's bullion program.

The services that the United States Mint provides to the American people are unique and valuable. I was fortunate to visit each Mint facility during 2019. The Mint staff at each of our field locations and our Headquarters in Washington, D.C. are a dedicated, motivated, and diverse group. I am honored to serve as their Director, and I look forward to continuing our forward progress in 2020 and beyond.

Sincerely,

David J. Ryder

ORGANIZATIONAL PROFILE

Seated left to right: Jennifer Warren, Director, Legislative & Intergovernmental Affairs; Andre Faulk, Acting Equal Employment Manager; Kirk Carter, Acting Chief Human Capital Officer; John Schorn, Chief Counsel; Matthew Holben, Associate Director, Sales & Marketing; Randall Johnson, Superintendent, Denver Mint; Ellen McCollum, Superintendent, West Point Mint; Kristie McNally, Chief Financial Officer

Standing left to right: April Stafford, Chief, Design Management; Thomas Johnson, Acting Chief Administrative Officer; Robert Kurzyna, Superintendent, Philadelphia Mint; Patrick Hernandez, Acting Deputy Director; David Ryder, Director, United States Mint; B.B. Craig, Associate Director, Environment, Safety, and Health; David Croft, Associate Director, Manufacturing; Bill Bailey, Deputy Chief, Mint Police; Eric Anderson, Executive Secretary

Not pictured: Joseph Jankauskas, Chief Information Officer; David Jacobs, Superintendent, San Francisco Mint; Todd Martin, Acting Chief Corporate Communications

OUR MISSION

The United States Mint (Mint) enables America's economic growth and stability by protecting assets entrusted to us and manufacturing coins and medals to facilitate national commerce.

OUR CORE VALUES

The Mint is privileged to connect America through coins and medals, which reflect the remarkable history, values, culture, diversity, and natural beauty of our Nation. To maintain the Mint's reputation as one of the finest mints in the world, Mint employees are committed to undertaking their work according to the core values of service, quality, and integrity.

Established in 1792, the Mint is the world's largest coin manufacturer. Since Fiscal Year (FY) 1996, the Mint has operated under the Public Enterprise Fund (PEF) (31 U.S.C. § 5136). The PEF enables the Mint to operate without an annual appropriation. The Mint generates revenue through the sale of circulating coins to the Federal Reserve Banks (FRB), numismatic products to the public, and bullion coins to authorized purchasers. Revenue in excess of amounts required by the PEF is transferred to the United States Treasury (Treasury) General Fund.

The Mint operates six facilities and employs nearly 1,600 employees across the United States. Each facility performs unique functions critical to our overall operations. Manufacturing facilities in Philadelphia and Denver produce coins of all denominations for circulation. Both facilities also produce dies for striking coins. All sculpting and engraving of coin and medal designs are performed in Philadelphia. Production of numismatic products, including bullion coins, is primarily performed at facilities in San Francisco and West Point. All four production facilities produce commemorative coins as authorized by Federal laws. The United States Bullion Depository at Fort Knox stores and safeguards United States gold bullion reserves. Administrative and oversight functions are performed at the Mint Headquarters in Washington, D.C.

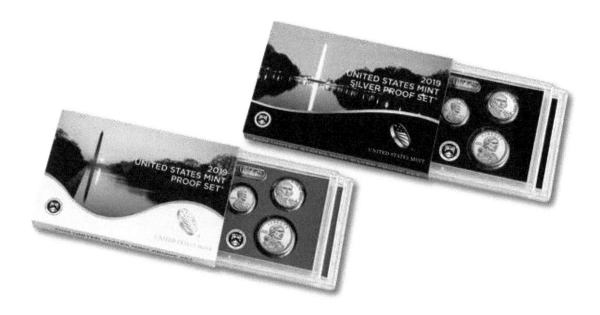

TABLE OF CONTENTS

THE UNITED STATES MINT AT A GLANCE

UNITED STATES MINT (MINT)

The men and women of the Mint manufacture and distribute circulating coins, precious metal and collectible coins, and national medals to meet the needs of the United States. The Mint has the following lines of operation: Circulating, Bullion, and Numismatic.

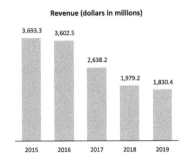

Revenue (dollars in millions)

2015	2016	2017	2018	2019
3,693.3	3,602.5	2,638.2	1,979.2	1,830.4

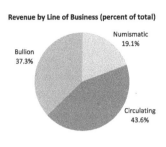

Revenue by Line of Business (percent of total)

Numismatic 19.1%
Bullion 37.3%
Circulating 43.6%

CIRCULATING COINAGE

The Mint is the sole manufacturer of legal tender coinage in the United States. The Mint's highest priority is to efficiently and effectively mint and issue circulating coinage.

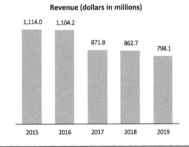

Revenue (dollars in millions)

2015	2016	2017	2018	2019
1,114.0	1,104.2	871.8	862.7	798.1

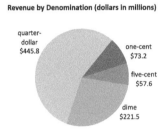

Revenue by Denomination (dollars in millions)

quarter-dollar $445.8
one-cent $73.2
five-cent $57.6
dime $221.5

BULLION COINS

The Mint is the world's largest producer of gold and silver bullion coins. The bullion coin program provides consumers a simple and tangible means to acquire precious metal coins. Investors purchase bullion coins for the intrinsic metal value and the United States Government's guarantee of each coin's metal weight, content, and purity.

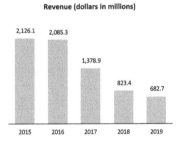

Revenue (dollars in millions)

2015	2016	2017	2018	2019
2,126.1	2,085.3	1,378.9	823.4	682.7

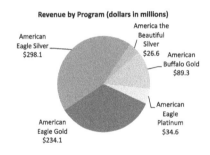

Revenue by Program (dollars in millions)

American Eagle Silver $298.1
America the Beautiful Silver $26.6
American Buffalo Gold $89.3
American Eagle Platinum $34.6
American Eagle Gold $234.1

NUMISMATIC PRODUCTS

The Mint prepares and distributes numismatic products for collectors and those who desire high-quality versions of coinage. Most of the Mint's recurring products are required by Federal statute. Others are required by individual public laws.

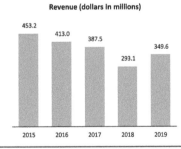

Revenue (dollars in millions)

2015	2016	2017	2018	2019
453.2	413.0	387.5	293.1	349.6

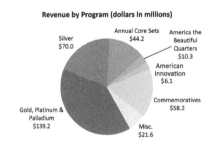

Revenue by Program (dollars in millions)

Silver $70.0
Annual Core Sets $44.2
America the Beautiful Quarters $10.3
American Innovation $6.1
Commemoratives $58.2
Gold, Platinum & Palladium $139.2
Misc. $21.6

SEIGNIORAGE AND NET INCOME

Seigniorage is the difference between the face value and cost of producing circulating coinage. The Mint transfers seigniorage to the Treasury General Fund to help finance national debt. Net income from bullion and numismatic operations can also fund Federal programs.

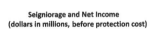
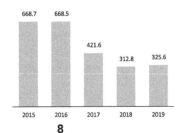

Seigniorage and Net Income (dollars in millions, before protection cost)

2015	2016	2017	2018	2019
668.7	668.5	421.6	312.8	325.6

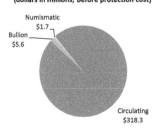

Seigniorage and Net Income by Line of Business (dollars in millions, before protection cost)

Numismatic $1.7
Bullion $5.6
Circulating $318.3

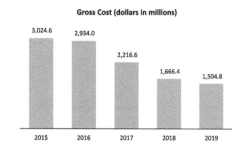

Gross Cost (dollars in millions)

3,024.6   2,934.0   2,216.6   1,666.4   1,504.8

2015   2016   2017   2018   2019

2019 PERFORMANCE

FY 2019 revenue was $1,830.4 million, a decrease of 7.5 percent compared to last year. Cost of goods sold (COGS) decreased 11.2 percent to $1,344.1 million. Selling, general and administrative (SG&A) expenses increased 5.0 percent from last year. Total seigniorage and net income before Protection expenses increased 4.1 percent to $325.6 million compared to last year, reflecting the impact of increased numismatic demand and lower metal costs.

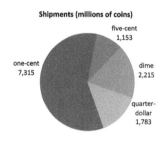

Shipments (millions of coins)

five-cent 1,153
one-cent 7,315
dime 2,215
quarter-dollar 1,783

CIRCULATING COINAGE

Circulating coin shipments decreased 8.8 percent to 12,466 million coins in FY 2019, driven by decreased shipments in all denominations. Circulating revenue decreased 7.5 percent to $798.1 because of lower dime and quarter-dollar shipments. Seigniorage decreased 0.9 percent to $318.3 million. Seigniorage per dollar issued increased to $0.40 from $0.37 last year.

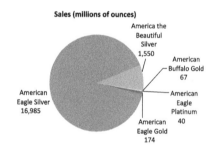

Sales (millions of ounces)

America the Beautiful Silver 1,550
American Buffalo Gold 67
American Eagle Silver 16,985
American Eagle Platinum 40
American Eagle Gold 174

BULLION COINS

Demand for bullion coins increased in FY 2019 compared to last year. The Mint sold 18.8 million ounces of gold, silver and platinum bullion coins, an increase of 3.6 million ounces from last year. Total bullion revenue decreased 17.1 percent to $682.7 million in FY 2019, primarily due to a 37.5 percent decrease in gold bullion coin revenues. Bullion coin net income decreased 20.0 percent to $5.6 million and bullion coin net margin decreased to 0.8 percent compared to 0.9 percent last year.

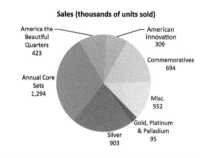

Sales (thousands of units sold)

America the Beautiful Quarters 423
American Innovation 309
Commemoratives 694
Annual Core Sets 1,294
Misc. 552
Gold, Platinum & Palladium 95
Silver 903

NUMISMATIC PRODUCTS

Numismatic sales increased 27.8 percent to 4.3 million units in FY 2019. Numismatic revenues increased 19.3 percent to $349.6 million due to a $6.9 million increase in annual core sets and $40.5 million increase in commemorative product revenues. Numismatic net income increased 111.1 percent to $1.7 million (before protection expenses). Numismatic net margin increased to 0.5 percent compared to (5.2) percent last year.

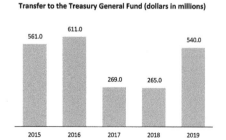

Transfer to the Treasury General Fund (dollars in millions)

561.0   611.0   269.0   265.0   540.0

2015   2016   2017   2018   2019

TRANSFER TO THE GENERAL FUND

In FY 2019, the Mint transferred $540 million to the Treasury General Fund from the United States Mint Public Enterprise Fund. The Mint transferred $540 million of seigniorage as a non-budget transfer. The Mint did not make a budget transfer in the first quarter of FY 2019.

MANAGEMENT'S DISCUSSION AND ANALYSIS (UNAUDITED)

CIRCULATING COINAGE FOR THE NATION'S COMMERCE

CIRCULATING

As America's sole manufacturer of legal tender coinage, the efficient and effective production and distribution of coinage is the Mint's highest priority.

The Mint produces and issues circulating coins to the FRB in quantities to support their service to commercial banks and other financial institutions. These financial institutions then meet the coinage needs of retailers and the public. The Mint recognizes revenue from the sale of circulating coins at face value when they are shipped to the FRB.

CIRCULATING RESULTS

FY 2019 circulating coin shipments to the Federal Reserve Bank decreased by 1.2 billion units (8.8 percent) to a total 12.5 billion coins compared to last year. Although the year saw decreases in all denominations, large decreases in dime and quarter-dollar shipments resulted in decreased revenue compared to last year.

The overall shipment mix remained approximately the same for all denominations compared to last year.

As a percentage of total shipments, nickels lost 0.5 percentage points to account for 9.2 percent of the mix in FY 2019. Dimes increased 0.4 percentage points to account for 17.8 percent of the mix. The quarter-dollars increased 0.4 percentage points to account for 14.3 percent of the mix. The pennies remained relatively constant as a percentage of total FY 2019 shipments, making up 58.7 percent of the total mix.

FY 2019 circulating revenue was $798.1 million, 7.5 percent lower than last year, driven by a $28.0 million (5.9 percent) decrease in quarter-dollar revenue. FY 2019 circulating seigniorage was $318.3 million, 0.9 percent lower than last year, due to reduced volumes. The resulting seigniorage per dollar issued was $0.40, $0.03 higher than the $0.37 last year.

FY 2019 unit costs decreased for the penny compared to last year. The unit cost for both pennies (1.99 cents) and nickels (7.62 cents) remained above face value for the fourteenth consecutive fiscal year.

Compared to last year, FY 2019 average spot prices for nickel decreased 1.6 percent to $12,937.41 per tonne, average copper prices decreased 9.1 percent to $6,072.91 per tonne, and average zinc prices decreased 15.2 percent to $2,607.23 per tonne.

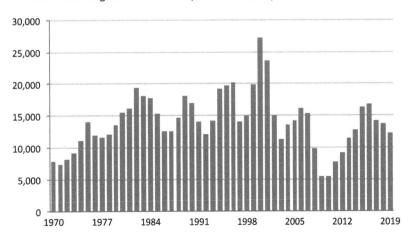

Total Circulating Coin Production (coins in millions)

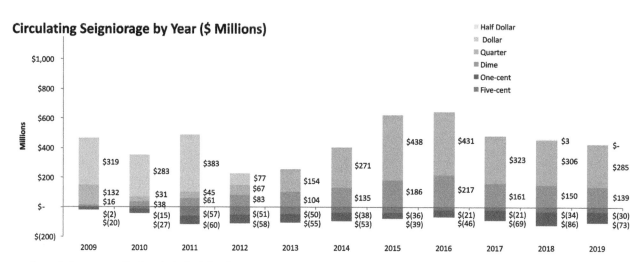

Circulating Seigniorage by Year ($ Millions)

Legend: Half Dollar, Dollar, Quarter, Dime, One-cent, Five-cent

Shows seigniorage generated by denomination for the last eleven years.

CIRCULATING
(coins and dollars in millions except seigniorage per $1 issued)

	2019	2018	2017	2016	2015	% Change 2018 to 2019
Coin Shipments	12,466	13,668	14,068	16,308	16,151	(8.8%)
Value of Shipments	$798.1	$862.7	$871.8	$1,104.2	$1,114.0	(7.5%)
Gross Cost	$479.8	$541.6	$480.3	$525.5	$573.1	(11.4%)
Cost of Goods Sold	$416.1	$480.3	$418.1	$468.5	$520.0	(13.4%)
Selling, General & Administrative	$63.7	$61.3	$62.2	$57.0	$53.1	3.9%
Seigniorage	$318.3	$321.1	$391.5	$578.7	$540.9	(0.9%)
Seigniorage per $1 Issued	$0.40	$0.37	$0.45	$0.52	$0.49	8.1%

UNIT COST OF PRODUCING AND DISTRIBUTING COINS BY DENOMINATION

2019	One-Cent	Five-Cent	Dime	Quarter-Dollar	Half-Dollar
Cost of Goods Sold	$0.0168	$0.0659	$0.0317	$0.0777	-
Selling, General & Administrative	$0.0029	$0.0095	$0.0051	$0.0114	-
Distribution to FRB	$0.0002	$0.0008	$0.0005	$0.0010	-
Total Unit cost	$0.0199	$0.0762	$0.0373	$0.0901	-

2018	One-Cent	Five-Cent	Dime	Quarter-Dollar	Half-Dollar
Cost of Goods Sold	$0.0178	$0.0659	$0.0323	$0.0778	$0.0526
Selling, General & Administrative	$0.0025	$0.0085	$0.0045	$0.0099	$0.0132
Distribution to FRB	$0.0003	$0.0009	$0.0005	$0.0010	$0.0000
Total Unit cost	$0.0206	$0.0753	$0.0373	$0.0887	$0.0658

2017	One-Cent	Five-Cent	Dime	Quarter-Dollar	-
-Cost of Goods Sold	$0.0156	$0.0564	$0.0284	$0.0711	-
-Selling, General & Administrative	$0.0024	$0.0088	$0.0045	$0.0103	-
Distribution to FRB	$0.0002	$0.0008	$0.0004	$0.0010	-
Total Unit cost	$0.0182	$0.0660	$0.0333	$0.0824	-

SHIPMENTS, COSTS, AND SEIGNIORAGE BY DENOMINATION
(coins and dollars in millions except seigniorage per $1 issued)

2019	One-Cent	Five-Cent	Dime	Quarter-Dollar	Half Dollar	Mutilated & Other	Total
Coin Shipments	7,315	1,153	2,215	1,783	-	-	12,466
Value of Shipments	$73.2	$57.6	$221.5	$445.8	-	-	$798.1
Gross Cost	$145.8	$87.9	$82.7	$160.6	-	$2.8	$479.8
Cost of Goods Sold	$124.9	$76.9	$71.3	$140.2	-	$2.8	$416.1
Selling, General & Administrative	$20.9	$11.0	$11.4	$20.4	-	-	$63.7
Seigniorage	$(72.6)	$(30.3)	$138.8	$285.2	-	$(2.8)	$318.3
Seigniorage per $1 Issued	$(0.99)	$(0.53)	$0.63	$0.64	-	-	$0.40

2018	One-Cent	Five-Cent	Dime	Quarter-Dollar	Half Dollar	Mutilated & Other	Total
Coin Shipments	8,057	1,327	2,381	1,895	8	-	13,668
Value of Shipments	$80.6	$66.4	$238.1	$473.8	$3.8	-	$862.7
Gross Cost	$166.1	$99.9	$88.6	$168.2	$0.5	$18.3	$541.6
Cost of Goods Sold	$145.7	$88.6	$77.9	$149.4	$0.4	$18.3	$480.3
Selling, General & Administrative	$20.4	$11.3	$10.7	$18.8	$0.1	-	$61.3
Seigniorage	$(85.5)	$(33.5)	$149.5	$305.6	$3.3	$(18.3)	$321.1
Seigniorage per $1 Issued	$(1.06)	$(0.50)	$0.63	$0.64	$0.87	-	$0.37

2017	One-Cent	Five-Cent	Dime	Quarter-Dollar	Half Dollar	Mutilated & Other	Total
Coin Shipments	8,426	1,306	2,410	1,926	-	-	14,068
Value of Shipments	$84.3	$65.3	$240.8	$481.4	-	-	$871.8
Gross Cost	$153.1	$86.3	$80.3	$158.7	-	$1.9	$480.3
Cost of Goods Sold	$133.0	$74.8	$69.5	$138.9	-	$1.9	$418.1
Selling, General & Administrative	$20.1	$11.5	$10.8	$19.8	-	-	$62.2
Seigniorage	$(68.8)	$(21.0)	$160.5	$322.7	-	$(1.9)	$391.5
Seigniorage per $1 Issued	$(0.82)	$(0.32)	$0.67	$0.67	-	-	$0.45

Base Metal Daily Official Spot Price (prices per metric tonne in dollars)

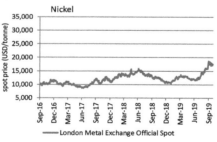

PRECIOUS METAL BULLION COINS FOR INVESTORS

BULLION COINS

The Mint's bullion coin program provides the public a simple and tangible means to acquire precious metal coins at a slight premium to spot market metal prices. Investors purchase bullion coins not only for their intrinsic metal value, but also because the United States guarantees each coin's metal weight, content, and purity.

The Mint produces and issues gold, silver, platinum, and palladium bullion coins to authorized purchasers through the American Buffalo, America the Beautiful Silver Bullion Coin™, and the American Eagle Programs. The Mint sells the coins to the authorized purchasers at the same market price paid for the metal, plus a premium to cover bullion program operating costs. Authorized purchasers agree to maintain an open, two-way market for these coins, assuring their liquidity. This allows the public to purchase and sell bullion coins at the prevailing market price, adjusting for any premium the authorized purchaser applies.

BULLION RESULTS

In FY 2019, the Mint sold 18.8 million ounces of bullion, an increase of 3.6 million ounces or 23.7 percent compared to FY 2018. Because of lower demand for gold bullion, FY 2019 bullion coin revenue and net income decreased compared to FY 2018. Revenue totaled $682.7 million, down 17.1 percent from $823.4 million last year. Net income decreased 20.0 percent to $5.6 million from $7.0 million, driven by lower American Eagle Gold and American Buffalo Gold bullion revenue, which decreased 33.2 percent and 46.5 percent, respectively.

In FY 2019, total demand for bullion increased from FY 2018 levels driven by increases in silver bullion coin ounces sold compared to last year; however, lower gold bullion ounces sold resulted in bullion revenue decreasing 17.1 percent below this time last year. Demand for gold continued to decline in FY 2019, just as it did in FY 2018. Gold ounces sold were 39.3 percent lower than in FY 2018, while gold bullion revenue decreased 37.5 percent compared to FY 2018.

GOLD BULLION COIN RESULTS

Bullion coin program results are highly dependent on trends in commodity market prices. These commodity prices are, in turn, dependent on variables such as global supply constraints, perceived strength as a safe-haven asset, currency exchange markets, and earnings potential from other commodities or investments.

The declines in gold bullion ounces that began during FY 2018 continued during FY 2019. Sales decreased 156 thousand ounces (39.3 percent) to 241 thousand ounces, with a 35.1 percent decrease in American Eagle gold bullion coin ounces sold compared to last year.

Gold bullion revenue decreased by 37.5 percent to $323.4 million because of decreases of 46.5 percent in American Buffalo revenue and 33.2 percent in American Eagle revenue, respectively. FY 2019 total gold bullion net income decreased by $1.4 million to $5.6 million (20.0 percent) below the $7.0 million in FY 2018. American Buffalo gold earnings decreased by $1.1 million compared to FY 2018 to $1.1 million. American Eagle gold earnings decreased by $0.3 million to $4.5 million compared to FY 2018.

The FY 2019 average daily spot price of gold was $1,329.04 per ounce, up 3.8 percent from $1,280.34 last year.

BULLION COINS
(dollars in millions)

	2019	2018	2017	2016	2015	% Change 2018 to 2019
Gold oz. sold (thousands)	241	397	693	1,018	1,018	(39.3%)
Silver oz. sold (thousands)	18,535	14,833	23,988	44,125	48,727	25.0%
Platinum oz. sold (thousands)	40	30	20	20	3	33.3%
Palladium oz. sold (thousands)	-	-	15	-	-	-
Sales Revenue	$682.7	$823.4	$1,378.9	$2,085.3	$2,126.1	(17.1%)
Gross Cost	$677.1	$816.4	$1,368.0	$2,030.0	$2,065.1	(17.1%)
Cost of Goods Sold	$662.9	$799.7	$1,342.7	$2,003.9	$2,038.5	(17.1%)
Selling, General & Administrative	$14.2	$16.7	$25.3	$26.1	$26.6	(15.0%)
Net Income	$5.6	$7.0	$10.9	$55.3	$61.0	(20.0%)
Bullion Net Margin	0.8%	0.9%	0.8%	2.7%	2.9%	(11.1%)

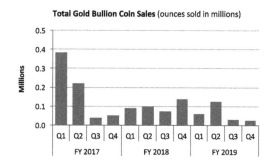

Total Gold Bullion Coin Sales (ounces sold in millions)

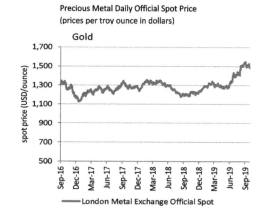

Precious Metal Daily Official Spot Price
(prices per troy ounce in dollars)

Gold

London Metal Exchange Official Spot

BULLION COINS REVENUE, COST, AND NET INCOME BY PROGRAM
(dollars in millions)

2019	American Eagle Gold	American Buffalo Gold	Sub-Total Gold	American Eagle Silver	America the Beautiful Silver	Sub-Total Silver	American Eagle Platinum	American Eagle Palladium	Total
Ounces Sold (thousands)	174	67	241	16,985	1,550	18,535	40	-	18,816
Sales Revenue	$234.1	$89.3	$323.4	$298.1	$26.6	$324.7	$34.6	-	$682.7
Gross Cost	$229.6	$88.2	$317.8	$293.7	$26.4	$320.1	$39.2	-	$677.1
Cost of Goods Sold	$228.3	$87.9	$316.2	$282.8	$25.3	$308.1	$38.6	-	$662.9
Selling, General & Administrative	$1.3	$0.3	$1.6	$10.9	$1.1	$12.0	$0.6	-	$14.2
Net Income	$4.5	$1.1	$5.6	$4.4	$0.2	$4.6	$(4.6)	-	$5.6
Bullion Net Margin	1.9%	1.2%	1.7%	1.5%	0.8%	1.4%	(13.3%)	-	0.8%

2018	American Eagle Gold	American Buffalo Gold	Sub-Total Gold	American Eagle Silver	America the Beautiful Silver	Sub-Total Silver	American Eagle Platinum	American Eagle Palladium	Total
Ounces Sold (thousands)	268	129	397	13,837	996	14,833	30	-	15,260
Sales Revenue	$350.4	$167.0	$517.4	$259.3	$17.1	$276.4	$29.6	-	$823.4
Gross Cost	$345.6	$164.8	$510.4	$256.1	$17.0	$273.1	$32.9	-	$816.4
Cost of Goods Sold	$343.5	$164.5	$508.0	$243.5	$15.8	$259.3	$32.4	-	$799.7
Selling, General & Administrative	$2.1	$0.3	$2.4	$12.6	$1.2	$13.8	$0.5	-	$16.7
Net Income	$4.8	$2.2	$7.0	$3.2	$0.1	$3.3	$(3.3)	-	$7.0
Bullion Net Margin	1.4%	1.3%	1.4%	1.2%	0.6%	1.2%	(11.1%)	-	0.9%

2017	American Eagle Gold	American Buffalo Gold	Sub-Total Gold	American Eagle Silver	America the Beautiful Silver	Sub-Total Silver	American Eagle Platinum	American Eagle Palladium	Total
Ounces Sold (thousands)	543	150	693	23,100	888	23,988	20	15	24,716
Sales Revenue	$694.9	$189.7	$884.6	$441.9	$17.2	$459.1	$20.6	$14.6	$1,378.9
Gross Cost	$683.2	$186.9	$870.1	$441.4	$18.1	$459.5	$22.5	$15.9	$1,368.0
Cost of Goods Sold	$679.6	$186.3	$865.9	$421.6	$17.4	$439.0	$22.2	$15.6	$1,342.7
Selling, General & Administrative	$3.6	$0.6	$4.2	$19.8	$0.7	$20.5	$0.3	$0.3	$25.3
Net Income	$11.7	$2.8	$14.5	$0.5	$(0.9)	$(0.4)	$(1.9)	$(1.3)	$10.9
Bullion Net Margin	1.7%	1.5%	1.6%	0.1%	(5.2%)	(0.1%)	(9.2%)	(8.9%)	0.8%

SILVER BULLION COIN RESULTS

Silver bullion ounces sold increased 3,702 thousand ounces (25.0 percent) to 18,535 thousand ounces in FY 2019, with a 22.8 percent increase in American Eagle silver bullion coin ounces sold and a 55.6 percent increase in America the Beautiful silver bullion compared to last year.

Net income from silver bullion coins increased 39.4 percent due to a $1.2 million increase in American Eagle silver earnings. America the Beautiful silver bullion coins experienced a $0.1 million increase (100 percent) in earnings compared to last year.

Higher volumes of silver bullion ounces sold meant that FY 2019 silver revenue increased by 17.5 percent. American Eagle silver revenue increased by $38.8 million (15.0 percent), and America the Beautiful Silver Bullion revenue increased by $9.5 million (55.6 percent).

The FY 2019 average daily spot price of silver was $15.50 per ounce, down 4.6 percent from $16.25 compared to the same period last year.

PLATINUM BULLION COIN RESULTS

From January 1, 2019 through May 31, 2019 the Mint sold a total of 40,000 ounces of American Eagle Platinum coins, 33.3 percent above the 30,000 ounces sold during FY 2018. As a result, revenue from platinum bullion in FY 2019 reached nearly $34.6 million, 16.9 percent higher than FY 2018 platinum bullion revenue. The platinum bullion program incurred a $4.6 million loss during FY 2019.

The FY 2019 average daily spot price of platinum was $842.97 per ounce, down 6.7 percent from $903.90 per ounce in the same period last year.

Total Silver Bullion Coin Sales (ounces sold in millions)

Precious Metal Daily Official Spot Price
(prices per troy ounce in dollars)

Silver

Total Platinum Bullion Coin Sales (ounces sold in thousands)

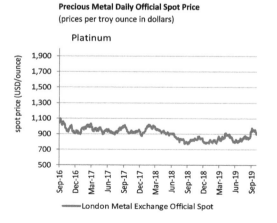

Precious Metal Daily Official Spot Price
(prices per troy ounce in dollars)

Platinum

U.S. MINT LAUNCHES APOLLO 11 50TH ANNIVERSARY COMMEMORATIVE COIN PROGRAM

On January 24, 2019, the United States Mint launched the Apollo 11 50th Anniversary Commemorative Coin Program, a unique four-coin program including the Mint's first reeded five-ounce proof silver dollar, a $5 gold coin, a silver dollar, and a half dollar. All the coins are curved, and this year, the Mint increased the silver content of its commemorative standard silver dollars to 99.9 percent silver. In the past, these coins were 90/10 silver—90 percent silver and 10 percent copper.

Gary Cooper of Belfast, Maine created the obverse (heads) design that appears on all the coins in this program. Cooper's design features the inscriptions "MERCURY," "GEMINI," and "APOLLO"—separated by phases of the Moon—and a boot print on the lunar surface. The design represents the efforts of the United States space program leading up to the first manned Moon landing. Additional inscriptions are "2019," "IN GOD WE TRUST," and "LIBERTY." Mint Chief Engraver Joseph Menna sculpted the design.

The coins' reverse (tails) design features a representation of a close-up of the iconic "Buzz Aldrin on the Moon" photograph taken July 20, 1969, showing just the visor and part of the helmet of astronaut Buzz Aldrin. The reflection depicted in Aldrin's helmet includes astronaut Neil Armstrong, the United States flag, and the lunar lander. Inscriptions are "UNITED STATES OF AMERICA," the respective denomination, and "E PLURIBUS UNUM." Mint Sculptor-Engraver Phebe Hemphill created and sculpted the reverse design.

The Half Dollar Set celebrates the connection between President Kennedy and the American space program. It includes one Apollo 11 50th Anniversary Proof Half Dollar and one Kennedy Enhanced Reverse Proof Half Dollar.

AMERICAN LEGION 100TH ANNIVERSARY COMMEMORATIVE COIN PROGRAM

In March 2019, the U.S. Mint released commemorative coins in honor of the American Legion's 100th Anniversary. The American Legion celebrates a century of providing dedicated services to the military, veterans, their families and the community. It is the nation's largest wartime veteran's service organization that continues to strengthen the nation through its advocacy, mentorship, and programs.

The American Legion 100th Anniversary Commemorative Coin Act (Public Law 115-65) authorized the minting and issuance of proof and uncirculated gold, silver and clad coins in recognition of the 100th anniversary of the American Legion. Designs were created by artists in the Mint's Artistic Infusion Program.

The $5 gold coin obverse design commemorates the inception of the American Legion and its mission to serve America and its war veterans. The outer geometric rim design from the American Legion emblem, the Eiffel Tower, and V for victory, represent the formation of the organization in Paris in 1919 at the end of World War I. The reverse design depicts a soaring eagle, a symbol of the United States during times of war and peace alike. The American Legion emblem is depicted above the eagle.

The silver dollar coin obverse design features the American Legion emblem adorned by oak leaves and a lily, commemorating the founding of the American Legion in Paris, France. The reverse design represents the founding of the American Legion in Paris in 1919. Above the crossed American and American Legion flags is a fleur-de-lis symbol and the inscription "100 Years of Service."

The clad half dollar obverse design depicts two children standing and reciting the Pledge of Allegiance, the little girl proudly wearing her grandfather's old American Legion hat. The reverse design features the phrase "I pledge allegiance to the flag… of the United States of America," along with a depiction of an American Flag waving atop a high flagpole. The American Legion's emblem is featured above the flag.

NUMISMATIC PRODUCTS FOR THE PUBLIC

NUMISMATIC

The Mint's numismatic program provides high-quality versions of circulating coinage, precious metal coins, commemorative coins, and medals for sale to the public. Most of the Mint's recurring products—such as United States Mint Uncirculated Coin Sets®, United States Mint Proof Sets®, and United States Mint Silver Proof Sets®—are required by Federal statute. Others, such as commemorative coins and Congressional Gold Medals, are required by individual public laws. A main objective of the numismatic program is to increase the Mint's customer base and foster sales while controlling costs and keeping prices as low as practicable.

NUMISMATIC RESULTS

Numismatic product sales increased to 4.3 million units in FY 2019 compared to 3.3 million units in FY 2018. The largest driver was increased sales volume in the commemorative coin product categories and the annual core set product categories. Commemorative coin product sales were 196.6 percent greater than last year. The Apollo 11 coin series was issued in January 2019 accounting for 82.3 percent of Commemorative product sales, contributing 13.4 percent of overall numismatic units sold during FY 2019.

In addition, the Annual Core set unit sales were 12.4 percent higher than last year. All three of the 2019 annual core sets increased in sales compared to their 2018 counter parts, contributing 22.9 percent to the overall numismatic units sold in FY 2019.

Numismatic revenue was also higher than last year. FY 2019 numismatic revenue was $349.6 million, a $56.5 million (19.3 percent) increase from FY 2018. There was a $40.5 million increase in revenue from commemorative coin products due to the issuance of the Apollo 11 coin series in January 2019 which generated $56 million and 413.8 percent more revenue than the 2018 World War I Centennial Silver Dollar, which was the highest revenue commemorative coin product in FY 2018.

The 2019 United States Mint Proof Set and the 2019 American Eagle Silver One Ounce Proof Coin were the most popular sellers (in terms of units) this year, selling a combined 725 thousand units. Sales for these products were 7.7 percent higher than they were last year.

Gold and platinum numismatic products generated the largest share of revenue (39.8 percent) during FY 2019 compared to the other numismatic products. This category generated $139.2 million in numismatic revenue compared to $210.4 million revenue generated by the other categories. Net income for FY 2019 increased 111.1 percent compared to FY 2018. Although, the annual recurring sets category recorded a $17.8 million net loss in FY 2019.

FY 2019 numismatic net margin was positive, increased to 0.5 percent in FY 2019 from (5.2) percent in FY 2018. FY 2019 numismatic COGS increased 13.6 percent by $31.7 million, driven by the increase in unit sales. SG&A expenses increased 10.4 percent this year.

Top Selling Products Fiscal Year
(units sold in thousands)

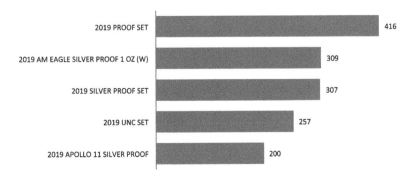

2019 PROOF SET	416
2019 AM EAGLE SILVER PROOF 1 OZ (W)	309
2019 SILVER PROOF SET	307
2019 UNC SET	257
2019 APOLLO 11 SILVER PROOF	200

U.S. MINT PARTNERS WITH INTERNATIONAL MINTS ON NUMISMATIC PRODUCTS

The Mint has initiated partnerships with several mints around the world to develop unique and interesting joint numismatic products. In January 2019, the Mint announced a collaborative project with the Royal Australian Mint. Together, the Mints produced a commemorative coin set in celebration of the historic Apollo 11 Moon Landing on July 20, 1969. The set features a U.S. Apollo 11 50th Anniversary Half Dollar paired with an Australian 50th Anniversary of the Moon Landing One Ounce $5 Silver Coin.

This limited edition set was sold and distributed by the Royal Australian Mint, and included a Certificate of Authenticity signed by the Director of the United States Mint and the Chief Executive Officer of the Royal Australian Mint.

The Mint also collaborated with the Royal Canadian Mint to produce a set featuring two iconic coins: the American Eagle One Ounce Silver Coin and the Canadian Silver Maple Leaf Coin.

We look forward to future collaborations with other mints worldwide to bring exciting new products to collectors.

NUMISMATIC
(dollars in millions)

	2019	2018	2017	2016	2015	% Change 2018 to 2019
Units Sold (Thousands)	4,270	3,341	3,905	4,159	5,379	27.8%
Sales Revenue	$349.6	$293.1	$387.5	$413.0	$453.2	19.3%
Gross Cost	$347.9	$308.4	$368.3	$378.5	$386.4	12.8%
Cost of Goods Sold	$265.1	$233.4	$302.5	$316.6	$322.3	13.6%
Selling, General & Administrative	$82.8	$75.0	$65.8	$61.9	$64.1	10.4%
Net Income & Seigniorage	$1.7	$(15.3)	$19.2	$34.5	$66.8	111.1%
Numismatic Net Margin	0.5%	(5.2%)	5.0%	8.4%	14.7%	109.6%
Seigniorage Portion	$8.6	$5.9	$10.2	$25.6	$26.0	45.8%

Net Income & Seigniorage figures are before protection costs. Seigniorage portion results from the sale of circulating coins (boxes, bags, and rolls) directly to the public through the numismatic channels.

COMMEMORATIVE COINS

Congress authorizes commemorative coins that celebrate and honor American people, places, events, and institutions. Although these coins are legal tender, they are not minted for general circulation. Each commemorative coin is produced by the Mint in limited quantity and is only available for a limited time. As well as commemorating important aspects of American history and culture, these coins help raise money for important causes.

In FY 2019, two commemorative coin programs were released – the Apollo 11 50th Anniversary Commemorative Coin Program and the American Legion 100th Anniversary Commemorative Coin Program.

The 2019 Apollo 11 commemorative coins had revenue of $56.0 million with surcharges of $8.4 million through September 30. This program runs through calendar year 2019 and final surcharges will be totaled December 31. The surcharges support the Astronauts Memorial Foundation and Astronauts Scholarship Fund.

The 2019 American Legion commemorative coins had revenue of $10.1 million with surcharges of $1.2 million through September 30. This program runs through calendar year 2019 and final surcharges will be totaled December 31. The surcharges are for the American Legion's programs supporting veterans and members of the Armed Forces.

NUMISMATIC REVENUE, COST, AND NET INCOME OR SEIGNIORAGE BY PROGRAM
(dollars in millions)

2019	Gold, Platinum, & Palladium Coin Products	Silver Coin Products	Annual Core Sets*	Quarter Products	Presidential & First Spouse Medals	Commemorative	Miscellaneous	American Innovation	Total
Units Sold (Thousands)	95	903	1,294	423	-	694	552	309	4,270
Sales Revenue	$139.2	$70.0	$44.2	$10.3	-	$58.2	$21.6	$6.1	$349.6
Gross Cost	$124.8	$53.9	$62.0	$15.4	-	$51.9	$31.2	$8.7	$347.9
Cost of Goods Sold	$121.4	$36.3	$35.5	$8.1	-	$39.3	$19.8	$4.7	$265.1
Selling, General & Administrative	$3.4	$17.6	$26.5	$7.3	-	$12.6	$11.4	$4.0	$82.8
Net Income & Seigniorage	$14.4	$16.1	$(17.8)	$(5.1)	-	$6.3	$(9.6)	$(2.6)	$1.7
Numismatic Net Margin	10.3%	23.0%	(40.3%)	(49.5%)	-	10.8%	(44.4%)	(42.3%)	0.5%
Seigniorage Portion	-	-	-	$2.1	-	-	$3.3	$3.2	$8.6

2018	Gold, Platinum, & Palladium Coin Products	Silver Coin Products	Annual Core Sets*	Quarter Products	Presidential & First Spouse Medals	Commemorative	Miscellaneous	American Innovation	Total
Units Sold (Thousands)	117	1,114	1,151	448	30	234	247	-	3,341
Sales Revenue	$132.8	$78.9	$37.3	$10.4	$1.2	$17.7	$14.8	-	$293.1
Gross Cost	$114.0	$76.1	$60.2	$18.7	$0.9	$17.8	$20.7	-	$308.4
Cost of Goods Sold	$110.5	$53.3	$32.7	$10.2	$0.5	$12.2	$14.0	-	$233.4
Selling, General & Administrative	$3.5	$22.8	$27.5	$8.5	$0.4	$5.6	$6.7	-	$75.0
Net Income & Seigniorage	$18.8	$2.8	$(22.9)	$(8.3)	$0.3	$(0.1)	$(5.9)	-	$(15.3)
Numismatic Net Margin	14.2%	3.5%	(61.4%)	(79.8%)	25.0%	(0.6%)	(39.9%)	-	(5.2%)
Seigniorage Portion	-	-	-	$2.2	$0.8	-	$2.9	-	$5.9

2017	Gold & Platinum Coin Products	Silver Coin Products	Annual Core Sets*	Quarter Products	Presidential & First Spouse Medals	Commemorative	Miscellaneous	American Innovation	Total
Units Sold (Thousands)	194	1,140	1,259	483	218	190	421	-	3,905
Sales Revenue	$216.2	$74.2	$41.8	$11.1	$12.4	$11.4	$20.4	-	$387.5
Gross Cost	$183.1	$62.1	$59.1	$14.8	$10.9	$12.5	$25.8	-	$368.3
Cost of Goods Sold	$176.7	$46.7	$35.9	$8.9	$7.5	$9.3	$17.5	-	$302.5
Selling, General & Administrative	$6.4	$15.4	$23.2	$5.9	$3.4	$3.2	$8.3	-	$65.8
Net Income & Seigniorage	$33.1	$12.1	$(17.3)	$(3.7)	$1.5	$(1.1)	$(5.4)	-	$19.2
Numismatic Net Margin	15.3%	16.3%	(41.4%)	(33.3%)	12.1%	(9.6%)	(26.5%)	-	5.0%
Seigniorage Portion	-	-	-	$2.0	$5.4	-	$2.8	-	$10.2

*Annual Core Sets are the United States Mint Silver Proof Set, United States Mint Proof Set, and United States Mint Uncirculated Coin Set.

COIN OF THE YEAR AWARDS

On February 2, 2019, United States Mint Director David J. Ryder accepted two awards on behalf of the Mint at the 2019 Coin of the Year (COTY) Awards competition at the World Money Fair in Berlin, Germany.

The American Liberty 225th Anniversary Gold Coin won in the Best Gold Coin category and the Boys Town Centennial Silver Dollar won Most Inspirational Coin.

"It is my great honor to receive the award for Best Gold Coin on behalf of the United States Mint," said Director Ryder. "The coin being recognized is truly special to our team. It was minted in 2017 to mark the 225th anniversary of the United States Mint. To observe this milestone, we proudly introduced the 2017 American Liberty 225th Anniversary Gold Coin featuring a modern rendition of Lady Liberty. This coin garnered a great deal of attention and sparked an interest in collecting for many who had never considered the hobby before."

"Honoring the Boys Town Centennial Silver Dollar as the Most Inspirational Coin speaks volumes about the ability of our artists to convey emotion—I am so proud of them," said Director Ryder after accepting the award. "I feel this coin represents America at its best—because we are truly at our best when we focus on helping others."

PEF EARNINGS AND TRANSFERS TO THE TREASURY GENERAL FUND

As required by 31 U.S.C. § 5136, the Mint deposits all receipts from operations and programs into the PEF.

Periodically, the Mint transfers amounts in the PEF determined to be in excess of amounts required to support ongoing operations and programs. The circulating, bullion, and numismatic program data exclude costs for the protection of custodial assets activity. Consolidated earnings are discussed below to provide a status of the entirety of the PEF compared to prior periods.

FY 2019 Protection costs decreased by 4.9 percent to $43.0 million compared to $45.2 million last year. FY 2019 PEF earnings after protection costs increased to $282.7 million compared to $267.6 million last year.

The Mint made one transfer to the Treasury General Fund this fiscal year totaling $540 million. The Mint can make two types of transfers to the General Fund. Non-budget transfers from the PEF consist of seigniorage, which is not treated as a budgetary receipt to the Government, but as a means of financing. Budget transfers to the Treasury General Fund from the PEF usually consist of numismatic net income and can be treated as a budgetary receipt to the Government.

In December 2018, the Mint did not make a budget transfer from numismatic and bullion earnings to the Treasury General Fund. On September 30, 2019, the Mint made a non-budget transfer of $540 million to the Treasury General Fund, compared to $265 that was transferred last year.

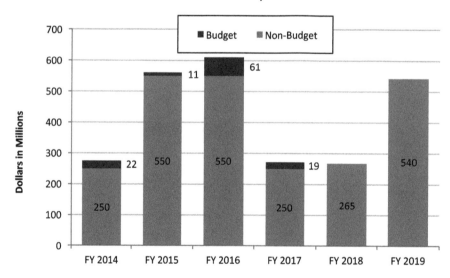

Transfer to the Treasury General Fund

HONORING AMERICAN INNOVATORS AND INNOVATIONS

In 2018, the Mint launched the American Innovation™ $1 Coin Program, a 15-year initiative to honor innovators and innovations from each state, the District of Columbia and the five U.S. territories—Puerto Rico, Guam, American Samoa, the U.S. Virgin Islands, and the Commonwealth of the Northern Mariana Islands.

Each year from 2019 through 2032, the Mint will release four new $1 coins with distinctive reverse designs in the order the states ratified the Constitution of the United States or were admitted to the Union. Once a coin is issued for each state, the Mint will release coins for the District of Columbia and the territories.

The common obverse (heads side) of all coins in this series features a dramatic representation of the Statue of Liberty and the required inscriptions "$1," and "IN GOD WE TRUST."

The reverse (tails side) design features an image or images emblematic of a significant innovation, an innovator, or group of innovators from one of the 50 states, the District of Columbia, or the territories; the name of the state, the District of Columbia, or territory, as applicable; and the required inscription "United States of America."

Coins in this series will display the year of minting or issuance, the mint mark, and "E PLURIBUS UNUM" on the edge of the coins.

The Mint issued a special American Innovation $1 Coin in December 2018 to introduce this exciting new series. The obverse of this coin features the same common obverse design as all the other coins in the series. The reverse design features a representation of President George Washington's signature on the first-ever U.S. patent issued on July 31, 1790.

FOSTER A SAFE, FLEXIBLE, DIVERSE, AND ENGAGED WORKFORCE

The Mint employees are at the heart of the organization's success; therefore, it is our goal to have a safe, engaged and innovative workforce. The Mint continues to promote employee awareness of safety protocols, improve training opportunities, and ensure compliance with applicable regulations and standards. The Mint has also embraced innovative practices by engaging modern technologies and becoming more environmentally sustainable, to not only benefit our employees, but also to benefit the American public.

ENVIRONMENTAL, SAFETY, HEALTH, ENERGY

Exposure to the chemicals used in the wastewater treatment process caused the injury of a Mint employee. The injury resulted in a lost time accident (LTA). This incident highlighted the extreme hazards associated with the concentrations of sodium hydroxide solution and hydrogen peroxide used in the treatment process. The Denver Mint used a 50% sodium hydroxide solution and a 35% hydrogen peroxide solution to address zinc and nickel anomalies in the treatment process. Both of these chemicals are extremely hazardous.

After extensive research and testing, the Denver Mint wastewater operations team eliminated both chemicals from the wastewater process and also eliminated the poisonous reagents containing cyanide used with testing for zinc. In addition to protecting employees from the hazards associated with these extremely hazardous chemicals, efficiency in the process was realized by eliminating the chemicals.

The Denver Mint has maintained perfect compliance with the industrial wastewater discharge permits. Along with this accomplishment, the wastewater operations team delivered extraordinary customer service to meet the needs of internal and external customers. This dedicated team worked wholeheartedly and tirelessly processing waste and reverse osmosis (RO) water while meeting all environmental regulations to render services exceeding customer expectations during the installation of a new automated wastewater treatment system.

In summary, the waste water teams' dedicated ability to process waste and reverse osmosis water positively contributed toward the production of quality annealed material the first time, reduction in scrap and rework, ensured final products met the Mint's highest standards and enabled the Denver Mint to meet all circulating and numismatic production goals.

UNITED STATES MINT EDUCATIONAL OUTREACH

The Mint's Education Outreach expanded its visibility this year with new lesson plans, interactive online games, and a fun-filled coloring book. The Mint fostered unique relationships with educators and enhanced academic enrichment through its combination of new education materials and increased participation at education events. The Mint also increased its exposure through its outreach efforts at educational conferences and classroom visits speaking directly with education professionals on ways to incorporate U.S. Mint resources into classroom curricula.

The Mint integrates coins into every lesson plan as a resource for educators to enhance learning and enrich the classroom. Educators have access to over 400 lesson plans designed for grades K-12 that support the concepts of National Curricular Standards in the subject areas of space exploration, astronomy, geography, history, language arts, mathematics, social studies, science, and other STEM-related fields. The flexible lesson plans also integrate technology into the core curriculum and support national education technology standards. The Mint's 11 online educational games connect lesson plans with classroom activity. The newest online games incorporate core academic subjects and coins to inspire learning skills. Space Supply, a fun space-themed game in honor of the 50th Anniversary of the Apollo 11 moon landing, allows players to deliver critical supplies to the Space Colonies across our solar system while dodging space debris, asteroids, and UFOs.

To enhance the learning curriculum through art, the Mint produced a new coloring book. New coloring pages highlight 2019 National Park Quarters, Commemorative Coin Programs, and spaced-themed coin designs. The downloadable 2019 Coloring Book features over 30 fun-filled pages of activities and coloring pages that feature Mint coin designs honoring important people, places, and events in U.S. history. There are over 100 downloadable coloring pages available to educators and parents.

MINT FACILITIES REACH KEY MILESTONES IN CONTINUOUS IMPROVEMENT

The Mint is a lean manufacturing organization that operates efficiently and employs cutting edge technology while observing the highest environmental and safety standards. This year, the engaged workforce in the Mint's facilities reached some key milestones in providing solutions to reduce Lost Time for Accidents and to promote a safe workspace.

The die manufacturing division at the Philadelphia Mint continued implementing the 6S process, improving the cleanliness and efficiency of the machine grinding work centers. The team removed more than 1,000 pounds of obsolete parts, tools, and steel cabinets, transforming the area to an organized workspace free of clutter.

The San Francisco Mint repaired and maintained its building and physical plant to keep operations safe, functional, and ready for production each day, including improvements for a new Police Division area, Employee Training Room, the Production Maintenance, and the EEO offices. San Francisco used the TAKE (TALK about the task; assess the ACTIONS; question your KNOWLEDGE; and, ensure having the right EQUIPMENT) TWO (the number of minutes it takes to think through the task) process before starting a job to save time and eliminate accidents.

The Denver Mint's Goal Diggers, one of the facility's safety teams, improved their safety culture and received the Director's award for their efforts in November 2018. The team revamped the Target Zero program, which recognizes Denver Mint staff for their safe work behaviors.

ANALYSIS OF SYSTEMS, CONTROLS, AND LEGAL COMPLIANCE

The Mint is responsible for establishing and maintaining effective internal control over financial reporting and has made a conscious effort to meet the internal controls requirements of the Federal Managers' Financial Integrity Act (FMFIA), the Federal Financial Management Improvement Act (FFMIA), Office of Management and Budget (OMB) Circular A-123, Management's Responsibility for Enterprise Risk Management and Internal Control, and the Government Accountability Office (GAO)'s Standards for Internal Control in the Federal Government. The Mint is operating in accordance with the procedures and standards prescribed by the Comptroller General and OMB guidelines.

The systems of management control for the Mint organization are designed to ensure that:

- Programs achieve their intended results;
- Resources are used consistent with overall mission;
- Programs and resources are free from waste, fraud, and mismanagement;
- Laws and regulations are followed;
- Controls are sufficient to minimize any improper or erroneous payments;
- Performance information is reliable;
- System security is in compliance with all relevant requirements;
- Continuity of operations planning in critical areas is sufficient to reduce risk to reasonable levels;
- Financial management systems are in compliance with Federal financial systems requirements, (i.e., FMFIA Section 4 and FFMIA);
- Complete and accurate data is reported on USASpending.gov; and
- Controls and policies are in place to prevent fraud and inappropriate use of government charge cards.

For all Mint responsibilities, unmodified assurance is provided herein that the above listed management control objectives, taken as a whole, were achieved by our organization during FY 2019. Specifically, this assurance is provided in accordance with Sections 2 and 4 of the FMFIA. The Mint further assures that its financial management systems comply with the requirements imposed by the FFMIA.

The Mint management is responsible for establishing and maintaining adequate internal control over financial reporting, which includes safeguarding of assets and compliance with laws and regulations. The Mint conducted the required Treasury assessment of the effectiveness of its internal controls over financial reporting in accordance with OMB Circular A-123. Based on the results of this assessment, the Mint can provide unmodified assurance that its internal control over financial reporting as of June 30, 2019, was operating effectively. No material weaknesses were found in the design or operation of the internal control over financial reporting. In addition, the Mint is committed to maintaining effective internal control, as demonstrated by the following actions:

- Annual audits of the Mint's financial statements pursuant to the Chief Financial Officers Act, as amended, including a) information revealed in preparing the financial statements, b) auditors reports on the financial statements, and c) internal controls and compliance with laws and regulations and other materials related to preparing financial statements.
- Annual performance plans, reviews, and reports pursuant to the Government Performance Results Act, which include analysis and evaluation of performance measures.
- The development, tracking, and closure of corrective actions identified in the Financial Statement Audit and OMB Circular A-123 Assessment.
- Internal management and program reviews conducted for the purpose of assessing management controls.
- Reviews of financial systems for requirements compliance in conjunction with OMB Circular A-123 and FFMIA.
- Reviews of systems, applications, and contingency plans conducted pursuant to the Computer Security Act of 1987 and OMB Circular A-130, Management of Federal Information Resources.

- Annual assessments, reviews, and reporting performed in compliance with the Improper Payments Elimination and Recovery Act of 2010 and the Improper Payments Elimination and Recovery Improvement Act of 2012 (IPERIA).
- Reviews and reporting in compliance with the Federal Information Security Management Act (FISMA).

The Mint continues to make improvement in maintaining effective internal control over financial reporting and is committed to monitoring and improving its internal controls throughout the entire organization.

LIMITATIONS OF THE FINANCIAL STATEMENTS

The principal financial statements have been prepared to report the financial position and results of operations of the Mint, pursuant to the requirements of 31 U.S.C. § 3515(b). The statements have been prepared from the books and records of the Mint in accordance with generally accepted accounting principles for Federal entities and the formats prescribed by the Office of Management and Budget. The statements are in addition to the financial reports used to monitor and control budgetary resources, which are prepared from the same books and records. The statements should be read with the realization that they are for a component of the United States Government.

UNITED STATES MINT COLLECTOR CARDS

This year, the U.S. Mint launched new, exciting Collector Cards as part of its robust education efforts to engage kids on coins and spark interest in coin collecting.

Each deck of six cards shows the cent, nickel, and quarter, as well as the Women Airforce Service Pilots, the Peter the Mint Eagle Coin Drop Game, and the new Mighty Minters™ character, Eli the Fox. The back of each card has fun facts and a QR code which points kids to the Mint's education site, where they can play interactive online games, learn more about coins, and download more resources.

Each deck has special cards that engage kids in coin design and coin collecting. The quarter card allows kids to insert a quarter of their choosing into an open slot in the card that holds the coin in place. The Women Airforce Service Pilots card and Eli the Fox card are lenticular cards, which show different images of the medal and character, respectively, when the kids shift the card while viewing it.

Kristie McNally
United States Mint
Chief Financial Officer

MESSAGE FROM THE CHIEF FINANCIAL OFFICER

As the Chief Financial Officer at the United States Mint, I am very proud to present the Fiscal Year 2019 Annual Report. I am also proud to report that the Mint's independent auditors have once again rendered an unmodified or "clean" audit opinion on these financial statements. I would like to take this opportunity to issue a heartfelt thank you to all of the dedicated men and women of the United States Mint for their hard work and attention to detail toward making Fiscal Year 2019 yet again an overall success with impressive results for our nation.

As the financial statements show, the Mint is in good fiscal health. Continued efforts to control costs, increase efficiency, and strategically reserve resources have provided a solid foundation that enables the Mint to be flexible when meeting coin demand as well as responding to our customers. Over the past several years, the Mint's continued efforts in lean practices, management controls, and cash management have positively affected the Mint's fiscal results. These efforts, combined with innovative products and partnerships have shown positive results for the Mint during Fiscal Year 2019.

The United States Mint's numismatic sales increased 27.8 percent to 4.3 million units in FY 2019. Numismatic revenues increased 19.3 percent to $349.6 million due to a $6.9 million increase in annual core sets and $40.5 million increase in commemorative product revenues. Additionally, numismatic net income increased 111.1 percent to $1.7 million (before protection expenses) and net margin increased to 0.5 percent compared to (5.2) percent last year.

During that same time period, circulating coin shipments decreased 8.8 percent to 12,466 million coins in FY 2019, driven by decreases in all denominations. Circulating revenue also decreased 7.5 percent to $798.1 due to lower dime and quarter-dollar shipments. Overall seigniorage decreased 0.9 percent to $318.3 million, however, seigniorage per dollar issued increased to $0.40 from $0.37 last year.

Demand for bullion coins increased in FY 2019 compared to last year. The Mint sold 18.8 million ounces of gold, silver and platinum bullion coins, an increase of 3.6 million ounces from last year. Total bullion revenue decreased 17.1 percent to $682.7 million in FY 2019, primarily due to a 37.5 percent decrease in gold bullion coin revenues. Additionally, Bullion coin net income decreased 20.0 percent to $5.6 million and bullion coin net margin decreased to 0.8 percent compared to 0.9 percent last year. These decreases would be expected as silver bullion was a large portion of bullion products sold this fiscal year.

In commemoration of the 50th anniversary of the first manned moon landing on July 20, 1969, the Mint launched the Apollo 11 50th Anniversary Commemorative Coin Program in January 2019. This historic event is memorialized on the Proof Silver Dollar, Five-Ounce Silver Dollar, Proof Gold and Uncirculated Clad coins. In addition, a special set featuring an Apollo 11 Proof Half Dollar and a Kennedy Half Dollar with an enhanced reverse proof finish was also issued through the program.

The Mint also commemorated the American Legion's 100th Anniversary. The American Legion celebrated a century of providing dedicated services to the military, veterans, their families and the community. It is the nation's largest wartime veteran's service organization that continues to strengthen the nation through its advocacy, mentorship, and programs. The American Legion 100th Anniversary Commemorative Coins were issued in proof and uncirculated gold, silver and clad versions in recognition of the 100th anniversary of the American Legion

The statements presented herein comply with accounting standards issued by the Federal Accounting Standards Advisory Board (FASAB). The FASAB is designated by the American Institute of Certified Public Accountants as the standard-setting body for the financial statements of Federal Government entities, with respect to establishment of the United States Generally Accepted Accounting Principles. In addition, the Mint conducted a comprehensive assessment of the effectiveness of internal controls over financial reporting. Based upon the results of this review, the Mint can provide unmodified assurance that its internal controls over financial reporting are operating effectively in accordance with Office of Management and Budget Circular A-123.

We are proud that the Mint continues to be strong financially and remain dedicated to helping lead the Mint's efforts to operate in the most cost effective manner. We will continue to adhere to sound fiscal principles, look for ways to improve the financial results of operations, and invest wisely in support of our mission to serve our customers.

Kristie McNally

Kristie McNally, Chief Financial Officer

WEST POINT MINT MARK QUARTER RELEASED INTO CIRCULATION

On April 2, 2019, coinciding with its 227th anniversary, the United States Mint announced that it has released the first ever circulating coins with West Point mint marks. Throughout the remainder of the year, two million each of the scheduled 2019 America the Beautiful Quarters® (10 million in total) were minted at West Point. The first of these coins bearing W mint marks were mixed in with quarters produced at Philadelphia and Denver and shipped on April 1.

The announcement kicked off a program designed to spark a renewed interest in coin collecting. The release also tied in with the American Numismatic Association's National Coin Week (April 21-27) and paralleled a separate initiative that organizers dubbed "the Great American Coin Hunt."

The America the Beautiful Quarters released in 2019 honor Lowell National Historic Park (Massachusetts), American Memorial Park (Commonwealth of the Northern Marianas Islands), War in the Pacific National Historic Park (Guam), San Antonio Mission National Historical Park (Texas), and the Frank Church River of No Return Wilderness (Idaho).

KPMG LLP
Suite 12000
1801 K Street, NW
Washington, DC 20006

Independent Auditors' Report

Acting Inspector General
Department of the Treasury

Director
United States Mint:

Report on the Financial Statements

We have audited the accompanying financial statements of the United States Mint, which comprise the balance sheets as of September 30, 2019 and 2018, and the related statements of net cost, changes in net position, and budgetary resources for the years then ended, and the related notes to the financial statements.

Management's Responsibility for the Financial Statements

Management is responsible for the preparation and fair presentation of these financial statements in accordance with U.S. generally accepted accounting principles; this includes the design, implementation, and maintenance of internal control relevant to the preparation and fair presentation of financial statements that are free from material misstatement, whether due to fraud or error.

Auditors' Responsibility

Our responsibility is to express an opinion on these financial statements based on our audits. We conducted our audits in accordance with auditing standards generally accepted in the United States of America, in accordance with the standards applicable to financial audits contained in *Government Auditing Standards* issued by the Comptroller General of the United States, and in accordance with Office of Management and Budget (OMB) Bulletin No. 19-03, *Audit Requirements for Federal Financial Statements*. Those standards and OMB Bulletin No. 19-03 require that we plan and perform the audit to obtain reasonable assurance about whether the financial statements are free from material misstatement.

An audit involves performing procedures to obtain audit evidence about the amounts and disclosures in the financial statements. The procedures selected depend on the auditors' judgment, including the assessment of the risks of material misstatement of the financial statements, whether due to fraud or error. In making those risk assessments, the auditor considers internal control relevant to the entity's preparation and fair presentation of the financial statements in order to design audit procedures that are appropriate in the circumstances, but not for the purpose of expressing an opinion on the effectiveness of the entity's internal control. Accordingly, we express no such opinion. An audit also includes evaluating the appropriateness of accounting policies used and the reasonableness of significant accounting estimates made by management, as well as evaluating the overall presentation of the financial statements.

We believe that the audit evidence we have obtained is sufficient and appropriate to provide a basis for our audit opinion.

Opinion

In our opinion, the financial statements referred to above present fairly, in all material respects, the financial position of the United States Mint as of September 30, 2019 and 2018, and its net costs, changes in net position, and budgetary resources for the years then ended in accordance with U.S. generally accepted accounting principles.

Other Matters

Required Supplementary Information

U.S. generally accepted accounting principles require that the information in the Management's Discussion and Analysis (including Analysis of Systems, Controls and Legal Compliance, and Limitations of the Financial Statements) and Required Supplementary Information sections be presented to supplement the basic financial statements. Such information, although not a part of the basic financial statements, is required by the Federal Accounting Standards Advisory Board who considers it to be an essential part of financial reporting for placing the basic financial statements in an appropriate operational, economic, or historical context. We have applied certain limited procedures to the required supplementary information in accordance with auditing standards generally accepted in the United States of America, which consisted of inquiries of management about the methods of preparing the information and comparing the information for consistency with management's responses to our inquiries, the basic financial statements, and other knowledge we obtained during our audits of the basic financial statements. We do not express an opinion or provide any assurance on the information because the limited procedures do not provide us with sufficient evidence to express an opinion or provide any assurance.

Other Information

Our audits were conducted for the purpose of forming an opinion on the basic financial statements as a whole. The Director's Letter, Organizational Profile, Our Mission and Core Values, The United States Mint at a Glance, Message from the Chief Financial Officer, and Appendix I: FY 2019 Coin and Metal Products are presented for purposes of additional analysis and are not a required part of the basic financial statements. Such information has not been subjected to the auditing procedures applied in the audits of the basic financial statements, and accordingly, we do not express an opinion or provide any assurance on it.

Other Reporting Required by *Government Auditing Standards*

Internal Control over Financial Reporting

In planning and performing our audit of the financial statements as of and for the year ended September 30, 2019, we considered the United States Mint's internal control over financial reporting (internal control) to determine the audit procedures that are appropriate in the circumstances for the purpose of expressing our opinion on the financial statements, but not for the purpose of expressing an opinion on the effectiveness of the United States Mint's internal control. Accordingly, we do not express an opinion on the effectiveness of the United States Mint's internal control. We did not test all internal controls relevant to operating objectives as broadly defined by the *Federal Managers' Financial Integrity Act of 1982*.

A deficiency in internal control exists when the design or operation of a control does not allow management or employees, in the normal course of performing their assigned functions, to prevent, or detect and correct, misstatements on a timely basis. A material weakness is a deficiency, or a combination of deficiencies, in internal control, such that there is a reasonable possibility that a material misstatement of the entity's financial statements will not be prevented, or detected and corrected, on a timely basis. A significant deficiency is a deficiency, or a combination of deficiencies, in internal control that is less severe than a material weakness, yet important enough to merit attention by those charged with governance.

Our consideration of internal control was for the limited purpose described in the first paragraph of this section and was not designed to identify all deficiencies in internal control that might be material weaknesses or significant deficiencies. Given these limitations, during our audit we did not identify any deficiencies in internal control that we consider to be material weaknesses. However, material weaknesses may exist that have not been identified.

Compliance and Other Matters

As part of obtaining reasonable assurance about whether the United States Mint's financial statements as of and for the year ended September 30, 2019 are free from material misstatement, we performed tests of its compliance with certain provisions of laws, regulations, and contracts, noncompliance with which could have a direct and material effect on the determination of financial statement amounts. However, providing an opinion on compliance with those provisions was not an objective of our audit, and accordingly, we do not express such an opinion. The results of our tests disclosed no instances of noncompliance or other matters that are required to be reported under *Government Auditing Standards* or OMB Bulletin No. 19-03.

Purpose of the Other Reporting Required by Government Auditing Standards

The purpose of the communication described in the Other Reporting Required by *Government Auditing Standards* section is solely to describe the scope of our testing of internal control and compliance and the results of that testing, and not to provide an opinion on the effectiveness of the United States Mint's internal control or compliance. Accordingly, this communication is not suitable for any other purpose.

KPMG LLP

Washington, DC
December 5, 2019

37

DEPARTMENT OF THE TREASURY UNITED STATES MINT
BALANCE SHEETS
As of September 30, 2019 and 2018

(dollars in thousands)	2019	2018
Assets		
Intragovernmental:		
Fund Balance with Treasury (Note 3)	$879,289	$1,120,347
Accounts Receivable, Net (Note 4)	-	82
Advances and Prepayments (Note 5)	2,823	2,906
Total Intragovernmental Assets	882,112	1,123,335
Custodial Gold and Silver Reserves (Note 6)	10,493,740	10,493,740
Accounts Receivable, Net (Note 4)	11,564	9,037
Derivative, Asset (Note 19)	1,533	11,043
Inventory (Note 7)	365,152	377,694
Supplies	19,618	16,741
Property, Plant and Equipment, Net (Note 8)	196,637	195,876
Advances and Prepayments (Note 5)	3	1
Total Non-Intragovernmental Assets	11,088,247	11,104,132
Total Assets (Notes 2 and 14)	$11,970,359	$12,227,467
Heritage Assets (Note 9)		
Liabilities		
Intragovernmental:		
Accounts Payable	$261	$185
Accrued Workers' Compensation and Benefits	8,068	7,900
Due to the General Fund	1	1
Total Intra-governmental Liabilities	8,330	8,086
Custodial Liability to Treasury (Note 6)	10,493,740	10,493,740
Accounts Payable	24,379	47,137
Surcharges payable (Note 3)	9,741	4,280
Accrued Payroll and Benefits	19,244	17,987
Other Actuarial Liabilities	31,424	31,184
Unearned Revenues	2,610	898
Deposit Fund Liability	30	-
Total Non-Intragovernmental Liabilities	10,581,168	10,595,226
Total Liabilities (Notes 10 and 14)	$10,589,498	$10,603,312
Commitments and Contingencies (Notes 12 and 13)		
Net Position		
Cumulative Results of Operations - Funds from Dedicated Collections (Note 14)	1,380,861	1,624,155
Total Liabilities and Net Position	$11,970,359	$12,227,467

The accompanying notes are an integral part of these financial statements.

DEPARTMENT OF THE TREASURY UNITED STATES MINT
STATEMENTS OF NET COST

For the years ended September 30, 2019 and 2018

(dollars in thousands)	2019	2018
Numismatic Production and Sales		
Gross Cost	$1,022,704	$1,122,835
Less Earned Revenue	(1,021,460)	(1,108,655)
Net Program Cost (Revenue)	$1,244	$14,180
Numismatic Production and Sales of Circulating Coins		
Gross Cost	2,040	1,912
Less Earned Revenue (Note 15)	(2,040)	(1,912)
Net Program Cost (Revenue)	$-	$-
Circulating Production and Sales		
Gross Cost	479,709	541,416
Less Earned Revenue (Note 15)	(479,709)	(541,416)
Net Program Cost (Revenue)	$-	$-
Net Cost (Revenue) Before Protection of Assets	$1,244	$14,180
Protection of Assets		
Protection Costs	43,006	45,218
Less Earned Revenue	-	-
Net Cost of Protection of Assets	43,006	45,218
Net Cost (Revenue) from Operations (Note 14)	$44,250	$59,398

The accompanying notes are an integral part of these financial statements.

DEPARTMENT OF THE TREASURY UNITED STATES MINT
STATEMENTS OF CHANGES IN NET POSITION

For the years ended September 30, 2019 and 2018

(dollars in thousands)	2019	2018
Cumulative Results of Operations		
Net Position, Beginning of Year - Funds from Dedicated Collections	$1,624,155	$1,608,102
Financing Sources:		
Transfers to the Treasury General Fund Budget	-	-
Transfers to the Treasury General Fund Non-Budget	(540,000)	(265,000)
Other Financing Sources (Seigniorage) (Note 15)	326,901	327,040
Imputed Financing Sources (Note 11)	14,055	13,411
Total Financing Sources	(199,044)	75,451
Net Cost from Operations	(44,250)	(59,398)
Net Position, End of Year - Funds from Dedicated Collections (Note 14)	$1,380,861	$1,624,155

The accompanying notes are an integral part of these financial statements.

DEPARTMENT OF THE TREASURY UNITED STATES MINT
STATEMENTS OF BUDGETARY RESOURCES

For the years ended September 30, 2019 and 2018

(dollars in thousands)	2019	2018
Budgetary Resources		
Unobligated balance from prior year budget authority, net	$730,755	$430,798
Spending Authority from Offsetting Collections	1,292,334	1,704,884
Total Budgetary Resources	$2,023,089	$2,135,682
Status of Budgetary Resources		
New Obligations and Upward Adjustments (Note 16)	$1,555,462	$1,424,770
Unobligated balance, end of year	467,627	710,912
Apportioned, unexpired accounts	467,603	710,910
Unapportioned, unexpired accounts	24	2
Total Budgetary Resources	$2,023,089	$2,135,682
Outlays, Net		
Outlays, net (total)	$241,089	($301,458)
Distributed offsetting receipts	(1)	(1)
Agency Outlays, Net	$241,088	($301,459)

The accompanying notes are an integral part of these financial statements.

NOTES TO THE FINANCIAL STATEMENTS

For the Years Ended September 30, 2019 and 2018

1. SUMMARY OF SIGNIFICANT ACCOUNTING POLICIES

REPORTING ENTITY

Established in 1792, the United States Mint (Mint) is a bureau of the Department of the Treasury (Treasury). The mission of the Mint is to serve the American people by manufacturing and distributing circulating, precious metal and collectible coins, national medals, and providing security over assets entrusted to us. Numismatic products include medals; proof coins; uncirculated coins; platinum, gold, and silver bullion coins; commemorative coins; and related products or accessories. Custodial assets consist of the United States gold and silver reserves. These custodial assets are often referred to as "deep storage" and "working stock," and are reported on the Balance Sheet.

The production of numismatic products is financed through sales to the public. The production of circulating coinage is financed through sales of coins at face value to the Federal Reserve Banks (FRBs). Additionally, the Mint sells certain circulating products directly to the public as numismatic items. Activities related to protection of United States gold and silver reserves are funded by the Mint Public Enterprise Fund (PEF). Pursuant to Public Law 104-52, Treasury, Postal Service, and General Government Appropriation Act for FY 1996, as codified at 31 U.S.C. § 5136, the PEF was established to account for all receipts and expenses related to production and sale of numismatic items and circulating coinage, as well as protection activities. Expenses accounted for in the PEF include the entire cost of operating the bureau. Any amount in the PEF that is determined to be in excess of the amount required by the PEF is transferred to the Treasury General Fund.

Treasury's Bullion Fund (Bullion Fund) is used to account for United States gold and silver reserves. Separate Schedules of Custodial Deep Storage Gold and Silver Reserves have been prepared for the deep storage portion of the United States gold and silver reserves for which the Mint serves as custodian.

BASIS OF ACCOUNTING AND PRESENTATION

The accompanying financial statements were prepared based on the reporting format promulgated by Office of Management and Budget (OMB) Circular A-136, Financial Reporting Requirements, and in accordance with accounting standards issued by the Federal Accounting Standards Advisory Board (FASAB). The Mint's financial statements have been prepared to report the financial position, net cost of operations, changes in net position, and budgetary resources, as required by 31 U.S.C. § 5134.

Management uses estimates and assumptions in preparing financial statements. Those estimates and assumptions affect the reported amounts of assets and liabilities, the disclosure of contingent assets and liabilities, and the reported revenues and expenses. Actual results could differ from those estimates.

Accounts subject to estimates include, but are not limited to, depreciation, imputed costs, payroll and benefits, accrued worker's compensation, allowance for uncollectible accounts receivable, and unemployment benefits.

The accompanying financial statements have been prepared on the accrual basis of accounting. Under the accrual method, revenues and other financing sources are recognized when earned and expenses are recognized when a liability is incurred, without regard to receipt or payment of cash.

EARNED REVENUES AND OTHER FINANCING SOURCES (SEIGNIORAGE)

Numismatic Sales: Revenue from numismatic sales to the public is recognized when products are shipped to customers. Prices for most numismatic products are based on the product cost plus a reasonable net margin. Bullion coins are priced based on the market price of the precious metals plus a premium to cover manufacturing, marketing, and distribution costs.

Numismatic Sales of Circulating Coins: Specially packaged products containing circulating coins are sold directly to the public rather than to the FRB. These products are treated as a circulating and numismatic hybrid product. Revenue is recognized when products are shipped to customers.

Circulating Sales: The PEF provides for the sale of circulating coinage at face value to the FRBs. Revenue from the sale of circulating coins is recognized when the product is shipped to the FRBs. Revenue from the sale of circulating coins to the FRBs and numismatic sales of circulating coins to the public is limited to the recovery of the cost of manufacturing and distributing those coins. Seigniorage is a financing source and not considered as revenue.

Other Financing Sources (Seigniorage): Seigniorage equals the face value of newly minted coins, less the cost of production (which includes the cost of metal, manufacturing, and transportation). Seigniorage adds to the government's cash balance, but unlike the payment of taxes or other receipts, it does not involve a transfer of financial assets from the public. Instead, it arises from the exercise of the government's sovereign power to create money and the public's desire to hold financial assets in the form of coins. Therefore, the President's budget excludes seigniorage from receipts and treats it as a means of financing.

Rental Revenue: The Mint sublets office space at cost to another Federal entity in a leased building in Washington, D.C. A commercial vendor subleases a portion of the first floor space of the same building.

FUND BALANCE WITH TREASURY

All cash is maintained at the Treasury. Fund Balance with Treasury is the aggregate amount of the Mint's cash accounts with the United States government's central accounts and from which the bureau is authorized to make expenditures. It is an asset because it represents the Mint's claim to United States government resources.

ACCOUNTS RECEIVABLE

Accounts receivable are amounts owed to the Mint from the public and other Federal entities. An allowance for uncollectible accounts receivable is established for all accounts that are more than 120 days past due. However, the Mint will continue collection action on those accounts that are more than 120 days past due, as specified by the *Debt Collection Improvement Act of 1996*.

INVENTORIES

Inventories of circulating and numismatic coinage are valued at the lower of either cost or market. Costs of the metal and fabrication components of the inventories are determined using a weighted average inventory methodology. Conversion costs (i.e., the cost to convert the fabricated blank into a finished coin) are valued using a standard cost methodology. The Mint uses three classifications for inventory: raw material (raw metal, unprocessed coil, or blanks), work-in-process (WIP – material being transformed to finished coins), and finished goods (coins that are packaged and bagged and ready for sale or shipment to the public or the FRB).

UNITED STATES CUSTODIAL GOLD AND SILVER RESERVES

United States gold and silver reserves consist of both "deep storage" and "working stock" gold and silver.

Deep Storage is defined as that portion of the United States gold and silver reserves which the Mint secures in sealed vaults. Deep storage gold comprises the vast majority of the bullion reserve and consists primarily of gold bars. Deep storage silver is also primarily in bar form.

Working Stock is defined as that portion of the United States gold and silver bullion reserves which the Mint can use as the raw material for minting coins. Working stock gold comprises only about one percent of the gold bullion reserve and consists of bars, blanks, unsold coins, and condemned coins. Similarly, working stock silver consists of bars, blanks, unsold coins, and condemned coins.

Treasury allows the Mint to use some of its gold as working stock in the production of gold coins. This allows the Mint to avoid the market risk associated with buying gold in advance of the sales date of the gold coins. The Mint replenishes the Treasury gold working stock at or just prior to the time the coins are sold. Generally, the Mint does not deplete the working stock used in production. Instead, the Mint will purchase a like amount of gold on the open market to replace the working stock used.

Treasury also allows the Mint to use silver as working stock. However, Treasury does not have enough silver to fulfill all Mint manufacturing needs. Accordingly, for the purpose of avoiding market risk associated with owning silver, the Mint has entered into a silver hedging arrangement (see Note 19).

SUPPLIES

Supplies are items that are not considered inventory and are not a part of the finished product. These items include plant engineering and maintenance supplies, as well as die steel and coin dies. Supplies are accounted for using the consumption method, in which supplies are recognized as assets upon acquisition and expensed as they are consumed.

ADVANCES AND PREPAYMENTS

Payments in advance of the receipt of goods and services are recorded as an asset at the time of prepayment, and are expensed when related goods and services are received or used.

PROPERTY, PLANT, AND EQUIPMENT

Property, plant, and equipment are valued at cost, less accumulated depreciation. The Mint's threshold for capitalizing new property, plant, and equipment is $25,000 for single purchases and $500,000 for bulk purchases. Depreciation is computed on a straight-line basis over the estimated useful lives of the related assets as follows:

Item	Depreciation
Computer Equipment	3 to 5 years
Software	2 to 10 years
Machinery and Equipment	7 to 20 years
Structures, Facilities and Leasehold Improvements	10 to 30 years

Major alterations and renovations are capitalized over a 20-year period, or the remaining useful life of the asset (whichever is shorter) and depreciated using the straight-line method, while maintenance and repair costs are charged to expense as incurred. There are no restrictions on the use or convertibility of general property, plant, and equipment.

HERITAGE ASSETS

Heritage assets are items that are unique because of their historical, cultural, educational, or artistic importance. These items are collection-type assets that are maintained for exhibition and are preserved indefinitely.

LIABILITIES

Liabilities represent actual and estimated amounts likely to be paid as a result of transactions or events that have already occurred. All liabilities covered by budgetary resources can be paid from revenues received by the PEF.

SURCHARGES

Public laws authorizing commemorative coin and medal programs often require that the sales price of each coin include an amount called a surcharge. A surcharge is an authorized collection and payment of funds to a qualifying organization for the purposes specified. A surcharges payable account is established for surcharges collected, but not yet paid, to designated recipient organizations.

Recipient organizations cannot receive surcharge payments unless all of the Mint's operating costs for the coin program are fully recovered. The Mint may make interim surcharge payments during a commemorative program if the recipient organization meets the eligibility criteria in the authorizing public law, if the recovery of all costs of the program is determinable, and if the Mint is assured it is not at risk of a loss. Additionally, recipient organizations must demonstrate that they have raised from private sources an amount equal to or greater than the surcharges collected based on sales. Recipient organizations must also prove compliance with Title VI of the Civil Rights Act of 1964 and other applicable civil rights laws. A recipient organization has two years from the end of the program to meet the matching funds requirement.

FUNDS FROM DEDICATED COLLECTIONS

Pursuant to 31 U.S.C. § 5136, the PEF was established as the sole funding source for Mint activities. The PEF meets the requirements of a fund from dedicated collections as defined in Statement of Federal Financial Accounting Standards (SFFAS) No. 43, *Funds from Dedicated Collections: Amending SFFAS No. 27, Identifying and Reporting Earmarked Funds*. As non-entity and non-PEF assets, the United States gold and silver bullion reserves are not considered to be funds from dedicated collections.

UNEARNED REVENUES

These are amounts received for numismatic orders which have not yet been shipped to the customer.

RETURN POLICY

If for any reason a numismatic customer is dissatisfied, the entire product must be returned within seven days of receiving the order to receive a refund or replacement. Shipping charges are not refunded. Further, the Mint will not accept partial returns or issue partial refunds. Historically, the Mint receives few returns, which are immaterial. Therefore, no reserve for returns is considered necessary.

SHIPPING AND HANDLING

The Mint reports shipping and handling costs of circulating coins and numismatic products as a cost of goods sold. General postage costs for handling administrative mailings are reported as part of the Mint's general and administrative expenses.

ANNUAL, SICK, AND OTHER LEAVE

Annual leave is accrued when earned and reduced as leave is taken. The balance in the accrued leave account is calculated using current pay rates. Sick leave and other types of non-vested leave are charged to operating costs as they are used.

ACCRUED WORKERS' COMPENSATION AND OTHER ACTUARIAL LIABILITIES

The Federal Employees' Compensation Act (FECA) provides income and medical cost protection to cover Federal civilian employees injured on the job or who have developed a work-related occupational disease, and to pay beneficiaries of employees whose deaths are attributable to job-related injuries or occupational disease. The FECA program is administered by the United States Department of Labor (DOL), which pays valid claims and subsequently seeks reimbursement from the Mint for these paid claims. The FECA liability is based on two components. The first component is based on actual claims paid by DOL but not yet reimbursed by the Mint. There is generally a two- to three-year time period between payment by DOL and DOL's request for reimbursement from the Mint.

The second component is the actuarial liability, which estimates the liability for future payments as a result of past events. The actuarial liability includes the expected liability for death, disability, medical, and miscellaneous costs for approved compensation cases.

PROTECTION COSTS

United States gold and silver reserves are in the custody of the Mint, which is responsible for safeguarding the reserves. These costs are borne by the Mint, but are not directly related to the circulating or numismatic coining operations of the Mint. The Protection Department is a separate function from coining operations and is responsible for safeguarding the reserves, as well as Mint employees and facilities.

OTHER COSTS AND EXPENSES (MUTILATED AND UNCURRENT)

Other costs and expenses consist primarily of returns of mutilated or uncurrent coins to the Mint. Coins that are bent or partial, but readily and clearly identifiable as genuine U.S. coins are classified as mutilated. The Mint reimburses the entity that sent in the mutilated coins using weight formulas that estimate the face value of these coins. Uncurrent coins are worn, but machine-countable, and their genuineness and denominations are still recognizable.

Uncurrent coins are replaced with new coins of the same denomination by the FRBs. The FRBs then seek replacement coins from the Mint. All mutilated or uncurrent coins received by the Mint are defaced and subsequently sold to its fabrication contractors to be processed into coils or blanks to be used in future coin production.

TAX EXEMPT STATUS

As a bureau of the Federal Government, the Mint is exempt from all taxes imposed by any governing body, whether it is a Federal, state, commonwealth, local, or foreign government.

CONCENTRATIONS

The Mint purchases the coil and blanks used in the production of circulating coins from three vendors at competitive market prices. The Mint also purchases precious metal blanks from four different suppliers.

CONTINGENT LIABILITIES

Certain conditions may exist as of the date of the financial statements that may result in a loss to the government, but which will be resolved only when one or more future events occur or fail to occur. The Mint recognizes a loss contingency when the future outflow or other sacrifice of resources is probable and reasonably estimable. Loss contingencies that are determined by management to have a reasonably possible chance of occurring or that cannot be estimated are included as a footnote to the financial statements. Contingent liabilities considered remote are generally not disclosed unless they involve guarantees, in which case the nature of the guarantee is disclosed.

TRANSFERS TO THE TREASURY GENERAL FUND

The Mint may transfer amounts determined to be in excess of the amounts required for bureau operations and programs to the Treasury General Fund periodically throughout the fiscal year. Seigniorage derived from the sale of circulating coins and the sale of numismatic products containing circulating coins is a non-budget receipt to the Treasury General Fund. Non-budget means that these funds cannot be used for currently funded programs or to reduce the annual budget deficit. Instead, they are used solely as a financing source (i.e., they reduce the amount of cash that Treasury has to borrow to pay interest on the national debt).

Revenue generated from the sale of numismatic products is transferred to the Treasury General Fund as a budget receipt. Unlike seigniorage, the numismatic transfer amount is available to the Federal Government as current operating cash or it can be used to reduce the annual budget deficit.

BUDGETARY RESOURCES

The Mint does not receive an appropriation from the Congress. Instead, the bureau receives all financing from the public and the FRBs, and receives an apportionment of those funds from OMB. This apportionment is considered a budgetary authority, which allows the Mint to spend the funds. The Mint's budgetary resources consist of unobligated balances, transfers, and spending authority from offsetting collections, which is net of amounts that are permanently not available. "Permanently not available" funds are budget transfers to the Treasury General Fund.

DERIVATIVE FINANCIAL INSTRUMENTS

The Mint engages in an economic hedging program to avoid the effects of fluctuating silver costs as a result of the changes in market prices.

The derivatives used for economic hedging in this program do not qualify for hedge accounting. At the time of purchase of silver inventory used in the production of silver coins, the Mint economically hedges its silver inventory using a silver forward derivative contract. The silver forward derivative contract is recorded in the Balance Sheets at fair value, with changes in fair value recorded in "Gross Cost" in the Statements of Net Cost. The silver forward derivative contract is settled as silver coins are sold to authorized purchasers, and a gain or loss is recognized, which is expected to substantially offset the gain or loss on the fluctuation in price of the silver inventory during that time the forward position remains open.

Each transaction with the trading partner carries a small transaction fee; the fees net to a cost of one-half cent per ounce. The Mint incurred $139 thousand in hedging fees in FY 2019, compared to $82 thousand incurred in FY 2018.

CLASSIFIED ACTIVITIES

Accounting standards require all reporting entities to disclose that accounting standards allow certain presentations and disclosures to be modified, if needed, to prevent the disclosure of classified information.

2. NON-ENTITY ASSETS

Components of Non-entity Assets at September 30 are as follows:

(dollars in thousands)	2019	2018
Custodial Gold Reserves (Deep Storage)	$10,355,539	$10,355,539
Custodial Silver Reserves (Deep Storage)	9,148	9,148
Custodial Gold Reserves (Working Stock)	117,514	117,514
Custodial Silver Reserves (Working Stock)	11,539	11,539
Total Non-entity Assets	10,493,740	10,493,740
Total Entity Assets	1,476,619	1,733,727
Total Assets	$11,970,359	$12,227,467

Non-entity assets are those that are held and managed by the Mint on behalf of the U.S. government but are not available for use by the Mint. United States gold and silver bullion reserves, for which the Mint is custodian, are non-entity assets.

3. FUND BALANCE WITH TREASURY

Fund Balance with Treasury at September 30 consist of:

(dollars in thousands)	2019	2018
Status of Fund Balance with Treasury		
Unobligated Balance Available	$467,627	$710,912
Obligated Balance, Not Yet Disbursed	411,662	409,435
Total	$879,289	$1,120,347

The Mint does not receive appropriated budget authority. The Fund Balance with Treasury is entirely available for use to support Mint operations. At September 30, 2019 and 2018, the revolving fund balance included $9.7 million and $4.3 million, respectively, in restricted amounts for possible payment of surcharges to recipient organizations.

4. ACCOUNTS RECEIVABLE, NET

Components of accounts receivable are as follows:

(dollars in thousands)	2019	2018
Intragovernmental		
Accounts Receivable	$-	$82
Total Intragovernmental Accounts Receivable	$-	$82
With the Public		
Accounts Receivable	$11,759	$9,257
Allowance	(195)	(220)
Total Public Accounts Receivable	$11,564	$9,037
Total Accounts Receivable	$11,564	$9,119

In FY 2019, the Mint had no Intragovernmental accounts receivable. In FY 2018, the Mint had an Intragovernmental accounts receivable balance of $82 thousand for services performed for another Federal Agency. Receivables with the public at September 30, 2019 are $11.8 million, of which $7.7 million is owed by fabricators for scrap, webbing, and mutilated coin. The remaining $4.1 million is owed by the public for numismatic products. This compares to receivables with the public at September 30, 2018, of $9.3 million, of which $8.0 million was owed by fabricators for scrap and webbing, in addition to the $1.3 million owed by the public for numismatic products. The allowance for doubtful accounts is the balance of the accounts receivable with the public that is past due by 120 days or more. Collection action continues on these accounts, but an allowance is recorded.

5. ADVANCES AND PREPAYMENTS

The components of advances and prepayments at September 30 are as follows:

(dollars in thousands)	2019	2018
Intragovernmental	$2,823	$2,906
With the Public	3	1
Total Other Assets	$2,826	$2,907

In FY 2019, the Mint had an Intragrovernmental advances and prepayment balance of approximately $2.8 million, which primarily represented payments made to the United States Postal Service for product delivery services as of September 30, 2019, compared to approximately $2.9 million paid at September 30, 2018. Advances with the public for both FY 2019 and 2018 are outstanding travel advances to Mint employees who were traveling on government business.

6. CUSTODIAL GOLD AND SILVER RESERVES

As custodian, the Mint is responsible for safeguarding much of the United States gold and silver reserves, which include deep storage and working stock. The asset and the custodial liability to Treasury are reported on the Balance Sheet at statutory rates. In accordance with 31 U.S.C. § 5117(b) and 31 U.S.C. § 5116(b)(2), statutory rates of $42.2222 per fine troy ounce (FTO) of gold and no less than $1.292929292 per FTO of silver are used to value the custodial assets held by the Mint.

The market values for gold and silver as of September 30 are determined by the London Gold Fixing (PM) rate. Amounts and values of gold and silver in custody of the Mint as of September 30 are as follows:

	2019	2018
Gold - Deep Storage:		
Inventories (FTO)	245,262,897	245,262,897
Market Value ($ per FTO)	$1,485.30	$1,187.25
Market Value ($ in thousands)	$364,288,981	$291,188,374
Statutory Value ($ in thousands)	$10,355,539	$10,355,539
Gold - Working Stock:		
Inventories (FTO)	2,783,219	2,783,219
Market Value ($ per FTO)	$1,485.30	$1,187.25
Market Value ($ in thousands)	$4,133,915	$3,304,377
Statutory Value ($ in thousands)	$117,514	$117,514
Silver - Deep Storage:		
Inventories (FTO)	7,075,171	7,075,171
Market Value ($ per FTO)	$17.26	$14.31
Market Value ($ in thousands)	$122,117	$101,246
Statutory Value ($ in thousands)	$9,148	$9,148
Silver-Working Stock		
Inventories (FTO)	8,924,829	8,924,829
Market Value ($ per FTO)	$17.26	$14.31
Market Value ($ in thousands)	$154,043	$127,714
Statutory Value ($ in thousands)	$11,539	$11,539
Total Market Value of Custodial Gold and Silver Reserves ($ in thousands)	**$368,699,056**	**$294,721,711**
Total Statutory Value of Custodial Gold and Silver Reserves ($ in thousands)	**$10,493,740**	**$10,493,740**

7. INVENTORY

The components of inventories at September 30 are summarized below:

(dollars in thousands)	2019	2018
Raw Materials	$97,468	$111,858
Work-In-Process	129,753	126,289
Inventory held for current sale	137,931	139,547
Total Inventory	$365,152	$377,694

Raw materials consist of unprocessed materials and by-products of the manufacturing process and the metal value of unusable inventory, such as scrap or condemned coins, which will be recycled into a usable raw material. In addition, as of September 30, 2019 and 2018, the inventory includes $124 million and $144 million, respectively, which are the market values of the silver hedged. Additional information regarding the derivative instrument can be found in Note 19. Work-in-process consists of semi-finished materials.

The Mint leases platinum and palladium to avoid the effects of fluctuating metal costs as a result of the changes in market prices. The Mint leases platinum for a fee that range between one to 1.2 percent of the asset's value and leases palladium for fees that range between four and 13 percent. The Mint takes physical possession of the metal to manufacture the bullion coins. Upon sale to the customer, the Mint purchases the metal from the lessor on the same day for the same market price. In FY 2019 and FY 2018, the Mint paid $412 thousand and $535 thousand in leasing fees for platinum. In FY 2019 and FY 2018, the Mint paid $1.5 million and $890 thousand in leasing fees for palladium.

8. PROPERTY, PLANT, AND EQUIPMENT, NET

Components of property, plant and equipment are as follows:

SEPTEMBER 30, 2019

(dollars in thousands)	Asset Cost	Accumulated Depreciation and Amortization	Total Property, Plant and Equipment, Net
Land	$2,529	$-	$2,529
Structures, Facilities and Leasehold Improvements	247,805	(160,239)	87,566
Computer Equipment	16,791	(15,623)	1,168
ADP Software	4,774	(4,699)	75
Construction-In-Progress	10,415	-	10,415
Machinery and Equipment	345,377	(250,493)	94,884
Total Property, Plant and Equipment, Net	$627,691	($431,054)	$196,637

SEPTEMBER 30, 2018

(dollars in thousands)	Asset Cost	Accumulated Depreciation and Amortization	Total Property, Plant and Equipment, Net
Land	$2,529	$-	$2,529
Structures, Facilities and Leasehold Improvements	229,642	(152,437)	77,205
Computer Equipment	19,590	(17,137)	2,453
ADP Software	4,774	(4,551)	223
Construction-In-Progress	16,657	-	16,657
Machinery and Equipment	338,610	(241,801)	96,809
Total Property, Plant and Equipment, Net	$611,802	($415,926)	$195,876

The land and buildings used to manufacture circulating coinage and numismatic products are owned by the Mint and located in Philadelphia, Denver, San Francisco, and West Point. In addition, the Mint owns the land and buildings at the United States Bullion Depository at Fort Knox. Construction-in-progress (CIP) represents assets that are underway, such as in the process of being readied for use, or which are being tested for acceptability, but which are not yet being fully utilized by the Mint and, therefore, not being depreciated. Depreciation and amortization expenses charged to operations during FY 2019 and FY 2018 were $27.2 million and $28.6 million, respectively.

9. HERITAGE ASSETS

The Mint maintains collections of heritage assets, which are any property, plant, or equipment that are retained by the Mint for their historic, natural, cultural, educational, or artistic value, or significant architectural characteristics. For example, the Mint's historical artifacts include, among other things, examples of furniture and equipment used in the Mint's facilities over the years, as well as examples of the coin manufacturing process, such as plasters, galvanos, dies, punches, and actual finished coins. The coin collections include examples of the various coins produced by the Mint over the years, separated into collections of pattern pieces/prototypes, coin specimens, quality samples, and exotic metal coin samples. The buildings housing the Mint's facilities at Denver, West Point, San Francisco, and Fort Knox are all considered multi-use heritage assets. The Mint generally does not place a value on heritage assets, even though some of the coins and artifacts are priceless. However, the assets are accounted for, and controlled, for protection and conservation purposes. The following chart represents the Mint's various collections and historical artifacts.

	Quantity of Collections Held September 30	
Coin Collections	2019	2018
Pattern Pieces/Prototypes	1	1
Coin Specimens	1	1
Quality Samples	1	1
Exotic Metal Coin Samples	1	1
Total	4	4

	Quantity of Collections Held September 30	
Historical Artifacts	2019	2018
Antiques/Artifacts	1	1
Plasters	1	1
Galvanos	1	1
Dies	1	1
Punches	1	1
Historical Documents	1	1
Multi-use heritage assets	4	4
Total	10	10

10. LIABILITIES NOT REQUIRING BUDGETARY RESOURCES

Components of Liabilities Not Requiring Budgetary Resources at September 30 are as follows:

(dollars in thousands)	2019	2018
Custodial Gold Reserves (Deep Storage)	$10,355,539	$10,355,539
Custodial Silver Reserves (Deep Storage)	9,148	9,148
Working Stock Inventory-Gold	117,514	117,514
Working Stock Inventory-Silver	11,539	11,539
Other	30	-
Total Liabilities Not Requiring Budgetary Resources	$10,493,770	$10,493,740
Total Liabilities Covered by Budgetary Resources	95,728	109,572
Total Liabilities	$10,589,498	$10,603,312

Liabilities not requiring budgetary resources represent the Mint's custodial liabilities to the Treasury that are entirely offset by United States gold and silver reserves held by the Mint on behalf of the federal government.

11. RETIREMENT PLANS, OTHER POST-EMPLOYMENT COSTS AND OTHER IMPUTED COSTS

The Mint received goods and services from other federal entities at no cost or at a cost less than the full cost to the providing federal entity. Consistent with accounting standards, certain costs of the providing entity that are not fully reimbursed the Mint are recognized as imputed cost in the Statement of Net Cost, and are offset by imputed revenue in the Statement of Changes in Net Position. Such imputed costs and revenues relate to business-type activities, employee benefits, and claims to be settled by the Treasury Judgment Fund. However, unreimbursed costs of goods and services other than those identified above are not included in our financial statements.

The Mint contributes seven percent of basic pay for employees participating in the Civil Service Retirement System (CSRS). Most employees hired after December 31, 1983, are automatically covered by the Federal Employees' Retirement System (FERS) and Social Security. A primary feature of FERS is that it offers a savings plan to which the Mint automatically contributes one percent of basic pay and matches employee contributions up to an additional four percent of basic pay. Employees can contribute a specific dollar amount or a percentage of their basic pay, as long as the annual dollar total does not exceed the Internal Revenue Code limit of $19,000 for calendar year 2019 (a $6,000 catch-up contribution can be given by participants age 50 and older in addition to the $19,000 contribution). Employees participating in FERS are covered by the Federal Insurance Contribution Act (FICA), for which the Mint contributes a matching amount to the Social Security Administration.

Although the Mint contributes a portion for pension benefits and makes the necessary payroll deductions, it is not responsible for administering either CSRS or FERS. Administering and reporting on pension benefit programs are the responsibilities of the Office of Personnel Management (OPM).

OPM has provided the Mint with certain cost factors that estimate the cost of providing the pension benefit to current employees. The cost factors of 38.4 percent of basic pay for CSRS-covered employees and 16.9 percent of basic pay for FERS-covered employees were in use for FY 2019. The CSRS and FERS factors were 37.4 percent and 16.2 percent, respectively, in FY 2018.

The amounts that the Mint contributed to the retirement plans and Social Security for the year ended September 30 are as follows:

(dollars in thousands)	2019	2018
Social Security System	$7,947	$7,685
Civil Service Retirement System	387	535
Federal Employees Retirement System		
(Retirement and Thrift Savings Plan)	16,470	15,824
Total Retirement Plans and Other Post-Employment Costs	$24,804	$24,044

The Mint also recognizes its share of the future cost of pension payments and post-retirement health and life insurance benefits for employees while they are still working with an offset classified as imputed financing. OPM continues to report the overall liability of the Federal Government and make direct recipient payments. OPM has provided certain cost factors that estimate the true cost of providing the post-retirement benefit to current employees. The cost factors relating to health benefits are $7,268 and $7,151 per employee enrolled in the Federal Employees Health Benefits Program in FY 2019 and FY 2018, respectively. The cost factor relating to life insurance is two-one hundredths percent (.02 percent) of basic pay for employees enrolled in the Federal Employees Group Life Insurance Program for both FY 2019 and FY 2018.

The amount of imputed cost related to retirement plans and other post-employment costs incurred by the Mint for the year ended September 30 is as follows (before the offset for imputing financing).

(dollars in thousands)	2019	2018
Health Benefits	$9,103	$9,092
Life Insurance	26	25
Pension Expense	4,360	3,688
Total Imputed Retirement and Postemployment Costs	$13,489	$12,805

In addition to the pension and retirement benefits described above, the Mint records imputed costs and financing for Treasury Judgment Fund payments made on behalf of the Mint. Entries are made in accordance with FASAB Interpretation No. 2. For FY 2019, the Judgment Fund paid $259 thousand on behalf of the Mint for the clean-up of an EPA Superfund site. The EPA Superfund payment was part of a multi-year court order, which requires that the Mint and four other federal agencies pay for cleaning up the site. Payments are made by the Judgment Fund when the judge in the case determines that the site owner has submitted valid bills for clean-up work. For FY 2018, there were no payments by the Judgment Fund on behalf of the Mint. Also during FY 2019 and FY 2018, the Mint received unreimbursed services (imputed financing) from another federal agency in the amount of approximately $308 thousand and $606 thousand, respectively.

12. LEASE COMMITMENTS
THE MINT AS LESSEE

The Mint leases office and warehouse space from commercial vendors, the General Services Administration (GSA), and the Bureau of Engraving and Printing. In addition, the Mint leases copiers and other office equipment from commercial vendors and vehicles from GSA. With the exception of the commercial lease on an office building in Washington, D.C., all leases are one-year, or one-year with renewable option years. The Headquarters building lease in Washington, D.C. has a term of 20 years with no renewal option years.

Future Projected Payments:	Non-Federal Leases
FY 2020	$10,582,640
FY 2021	9,948,251
FY 2022	10,191,987
FY 2023	10,446,152
FY 2024	9,820,791
After 5 Years	138,870,323
Total Future Operating Lease Payments	$189,860,144

THE MINT AS LESSOR

The Mint sublets office space at cost to another Federal entity in the leased Headquarters building in Washington, D.C. As of September 30, 2019, the Mint sublets approximately 4,500 square feet of office space to the U.S. Marshals Service. This sublease is an operating lease and subject to annual availability of funding. The Mint has also entered into agreements to sublet space in the Headquarters building to two commercial tenants.

Future Projected Receipts:	Non-Federal Building Sub-Lease
FY 2020	$529,349
FY 2021	744,996
FY 2022	746,557
FY 2023	755,971
FY 2024	765,667
After 5 Years	786,538
Total Future Operating Lease Payments	$4,329,078

13. CONTINGENCIES

The Mint is subject to legal proceedings and claims which arise in the ordinary course of its business. Judgments, if any, resulting from pending litigation against the Mint generally would be satisfied from the PEF. Likewise, under the *Notification and Federal Employee Antidiscrimination and Retaliation Act of 2002* (No FEAR Act, P. L. 107-174), settlements and judgments related to acts of discrimination and retaliation for whistle-blowing will be paid from the PEF.

The Mint is also involved in employment related legal actions (e.g., matters alleging discrimination and other claims before federal courts, the Equal Employment Opportunity Commission, and the Merit Systems Protection Board) for which an unfavorable outcome is reasonably possible, but for which an estimate of potential loss cannot be determined at this time. In the opinion of management, the ultimate resolution of these actions will not have a material adverse effect on the Mint's financial position or the results of its operations.

14. FUNDS FROM DEDICATED COLLECTIONS

Pursuant to 31 U.S.C. § 5136, all receipts from Mint operations and programs, including the production and sale of numismatic items, the production and sale of circulating coinage at face value to the FRB, the protection of government assets, and gifts and bequests of property, real or personal shall be deposited into the PEF and shall be available to fund its operations without fiscal year limitations.

The PEF meets the requirements of funds from dedicated collections as defined in SFFAS No. 43, *Funds from Dedicated Collections: Amending SFFAS No. 27, Identifying and Reporting Earmarked Funds.* As non-entity and non-PEF assets, the United States gold and silver reserves are not included in the funds from dedicated collections.

15. EARNED REVENUE AND OTHER FINANCING SOURCES (SEIGNIORAGE)

The Statement of Net Cost reflects the earned revenue and corresponding gross costs for Circulating Production and Sales and for Numismatic Production and Sales of Circulating Coins. Circulating Production and Sales represents coin sales to the FRB, and Numismatic Production and Sales of Circulating Coins represents sales of circulating coins to the public (i.e., numismatic customers).

SFFAS No. 7, Accounting for Revenue and Other Financing Sources and Concepts for Reconciling Budgetary and Financial Accounting, provides requirements related to the recognition of net program revenue from production of circulating coins to the cost of metal, manufacturing and transportation. OMB Circular A-136 defines the treatment of other financing sources on the Statement of Changes in Net Position, particularly as it relates to seigniorage. Therefore, on the Statement of Net Cost, earned revenue is recognized only to the extent of the gross cost of production. The difference between those costs and the face value of the coin is an "Other Financing Sources" referred to as seigniorage. Any revenue over face value for circulating coins sold as numismatic items is considered earned revenue and included in the category Numismatic Production and Sales on the Statement of Net Cost.

The following chart reflects the two components of the receipts from the sale of circulating coin – the earned revenue from the Statements of Net Cost and Seigniorage from the Statements of Changes in Net Position for the years ended September 30:

(dollars in thousands)	2019	2018
Revenue - FRB	$479,709	$541,416
Seigniorage - FRB	318,278	321,120
Total Circulating Coins	$797,987	$862,536
Revenue - with the public	$2,040	$1,912
Seigniorage - with the public	8,623	5,920
Total Numismatic sales of Circulating Coins	$10,663	$7,832
Total Seigniorage	$326,901	$327,040

16. APPORTIONMENT CATEGORIES OF OBLIGATIONS INCURRED

The Mint receives apportionments of its resources from OMB. An apportionment is an OMB-approved plan to use budgetary resources. An apportionment typically limits the obligations an agency may incur for specified time periods, programs, activities, projects, objects, or any combination thereof. All Mint obligations are classified as reimbursable, as they are financed by offsetting collections received in return for goods and services provided. OMB uses several categories to distribute budgetary resources. Category B apportions budgetary resources by program, project, activities, objects or a combination of these categories. The Mint had only category B apportionments in FY 2019 and FY 2018.

The following chart reflects the amount of reimbursable obligations incurred against amounts apportioned under categories B apportionments.

(dollars in thousands)	2019	2018
Category B		
Total Operating Expenses	$1,517,144	$1,385,696
Numismatic Capital	10,139	10,365
Circulating and Protection Capital	28,179	28,709
Total Apportionment Categories of Obligations Incurred	$1,555,462	$1,424,770

17. EXPLANATION OF DIFFERENCES BETWEEN THE STATEMENT OF BUDGETARY RESOURCES AND THE BUDGET OF THE UNITED STATES GOVERNMENT

SFFAS No. 7, *Accounting for Revenue and Other Financing Sources and Concepts for Reconciling Budgetary and Financial Accounting*, requires an explanation of material differences between the Statement of Budgetary Resources (SBR) and the related actual balances published in the Budget of the United States Government (President's Budget). The President's Budget with actual numbers for FY 2019 is expected to be published in February 2020 and made available through OMB. Therefore, the analysis presented here is for the prior year (FY 2018) "actual" figures published in the President's budget in February 2019. The following chart displays the comparison of the FY 2018 SBR and the actual FY 2018 balances included in the FY 2020 President's Budget. The differences between the FY 2018 SBR and the President's Budget is as a result of the headquarters building lease obligation from the prior year being adjusted to the present value of the obligation at year end.

(rounded to millions)   September 30, 2018

United States Public Enterprise Fund	Statement of Budgetary Resources	President's Budget	Difference
Budgetary Resources	$2,136	$2,147	($11)
New Obligations Incurred and Upward Adjustments	$1,425	$1,425	$-
Net Outlays	($301)	($301)	$-

18. LEGAL ARRANGEMENTS AFFECTING USE OF UNOBLIGATED BALANCES

The PEF statute establishes that all receipts from Mint operations and programs, including the production and sale of numismatic items, the production and sale of circulating coinage, the protection of government assets, and gifts and bequests of property, real or personal, shall be deposited into the PEF and shall be available without fiscal year limitations. Any amount that the Secretary of the Treasury determines to be in excess of the amount required by the PEF shall be transferred to the Treasury for deposit as miscellaneous receipts. At September 30, 2019 and 2018, the Mint transferred excess receipts to the Treasury General Fund of $540 million and $265 million, respectively.

19. DERIVATIVE FINANCIAL INSTRUMENTS

At September 30, 2019 and 2018, the fair value of the silver forward contracts were an asset of $1.5 million and $11 million, respectively, which are located in "Derivative, Asset", in the Balance Sheets. The Mint recorded net gains of $11.8 million on its silver forward contract in FY 2019, compared to net gains of $23.4 million in FY 2018, located in "Gross Cost" in the Statements of Net Cost.

20. RECONCILIATION OF NET COST TO NET OUTLAYS

The Reconciliation of Net Cost to Net Outlays depicts the difference between budgetary and proprietary accounting information. Budgetary accounting is used for planning and control purposes and relates to both the receipt and use of cash, as well as reporting the federal deficit. Proprietary accounting is intended to provide a picture of the U.S. government's financial operations and financial position, so it presents information on an accrual basis in accordance with U.S. GAAP, which includes information about costs arising from the consumption of assets and the incurrence of liabilities. The reconciliation of Net Outlays (presented on a budgetary basis) and the Net Cost (presented on an accrual basis) provides an explanation of the relationship between budgetary and proprietary accounting information. The reconciliation serves not only to identify costs paid for in the past and those that will be paid in the future, but also to assure integrity between budgetary and proprietary accounting. The analysis below illustrates this reconciliation by listing the key difference between net cost and net outlays:

Contra seigniorage in the reconciliation is a result of the difference between the seigniorage generated in FY 2019 and the non-budget transfer to the Treasury General Fund. The non-budget transfer to the Treasury General Fund did not result in a cost, but did result in an outlay. This number is positive as a result of transferring more seigniorage to the Treasury General Fund than was generated in FY 2019.

	September 30, 2019		
(dollars in thousands)	Intra-governmental	With the Public	Total FY 2019
Net Operating Cost (SNC)	$81,406	($37,156)	$44,250
Components of Net Cost That Are Not Part of Net Outlays			
Property, plant, and equipment depreciation	-	(27,158)	(27,158)
Property, plant, and equipment disposal & reevaluation	-	(43)	(43)
Contra seigniorage	-	213,099	213,099
Increase/(decrease) in assets:			
Accounts receivable	(82)	2,527	2,445
Other assets	(84)	(19,172)	(19,256)
(Increase)/decrease in liabilities			
Accounts payable	(76)	21,046	20,970
Salaries and benefits	(168)	(1,256)	(1,424)
Other liabilities	-	(5,701)	(5,701)
Other financing sources:			
Federal employee retirement benefit costs paid by OPM and imputed to the agency	(14,055)	-	(14,055)
Total Components of Net Cost That Are Not Part of Net Outlays	($14,465)	$183,342	$168,877
Components of Net Outlays That Are Not Part of Net Cost			
Acquisition of capital assets	-	27,962	27,962
Total Components of Net Outlays That Are Not Part of Net Cost	-	$27,962	$27,962
Net Outlays (Calculated Total)	$66,941	$174,148	$241,089
Related Amounts on the Statement of Budgetary Resources			
Outlays, net, (total)			241,089
Distributed offsetting receipts			(1)
Outlays, Net			$241,088

21. UNDELIVERED ORDERS AT THE END OF THE PERIOD

Undelivered orders represent goods and services ordered and obligated which have not been received. This includes any orders for which we have paid in advance, but for which delivery or performance has not yet occurred.

	September 30, 2019		
(dollars in thousands)	Federal	Non-Federal	Total
Paid	$2,823	$3	$2,826
Unpaid	2,956	325,513	328,469
Undelivered Orders at the End of the Year	$5,779	$325,516	$331,295

	September 30, 2018		
(dollars in thousands)	Federal	Non-Federal	Total
Paid	$2,906	$1	$2,907
Unpaid	3,026	290,384	293,410
Undelivered Orders at the End of the Year	$5,932	$290,385	$296,317

22. NET ADJUSTMENT TO UNOBLIGATED BALANCE, BROUGHT FORWARD OCTOBER 1

During the year ended September 30, 2019, certain adjustments were made to the balance of unobligated budgetary resources available as of October 1, 2018, located in the Statement of Budgetary Resources. These adjustments include downward adjustments to undelivered and delivered orders that were obligated in a prior fiscal year. These downward adjustments increased the unobligated balance of budgetary resources available as of October 1, 2018. The adjustments during the year ended September 30, 2019 are presented below.

(dollars in thousands)	
Unobligated balance, brought forward from prior year	$710,912
Downward adjustments of prior year undelivered and delivered orders made during current year	$19,843
Unobligated balance from prior year budget authority, net	$730,755

REQUIRED SUPPLEMENTARY INFORMATION (UNAUDITED)

FOR THE YEARS ENDED SEPTEMBER 30, 2019 AND 2018

INTRODUCTION

This section provides the Required Supplementary Information as prescribed by the OMB Circular A-136, *Financial Reporting Requirements, SFFAS No. 29, Heritage Assets and Stewardship Land and SFFAS No. 42, Deferred Maintenance and Repairs: Amending SFFAS Nos. 6, 14, 29 and 32.*

HERITAGE ASSETS

The Mint is steward of a large, unique and diversified body of heritage assets that demonstrate the social, educational, and cultural heritage of the Mint. These items include a variety of rare and semi-precious coin collections and historical artifacts, and are held at various Mint locations. Some of these items are placed in locked vaults within the Mint, where access is limited to only special authorized personnel. Other items are on full display to the public, requiring little if any authorization to view.

Included in the heritage assets are the buildings housing the Mint at Denver, West Point, San Francisco, and Fort Knox. The Mint generally does not place a value on heritage assets, even though some of the coins and artifacts are priceless. However, the assets are accounted for, and controlled, for protection and conservation purposes. Heritage assets held by the Mint are generally in acceptable physical condition.

DEFERRED MAINTENANCE

Deferred maintenance and repairs is maintenance and repair activity that was not performed when it should have been, or was scheduled to be, and is put off or delayed for a future period. In fiscal years 2019 and 2018, the Mint had no deferred maintenance costs to report on vehicles, buildings, structures, and equipment owned by the Mint. There is also no deferred maintenance on heritage assets, which includes the Denver, West Point, San Francisco, and Fort Knox buildings.

APPENDIX: FY 2019 COIN AND MEDAL PRODUCTS

AMERICA THE BEAUTIFUL QUARTERS® PROGRAM

BLOCK ISLAND NATIONAL WILDLIFE REFUGE QUARTER – RHODE ISLAND

Released for Sale: November 13, 2018

Description: Block Island National Wildlife Refuge is located 12 miles off the southern coast of Rhode Island and sits on a terminal moraine shaped by glacial till deposits creating rolling dunes. These wild lands are known internationally for spectacular bird watching and breathtaking barrier beaches. The reverse design depicts a black-crowned night-heron flying over a view from the beach at Cow Cove looking towards Sandy Point. The North Light lighthouse is seen in the background.

LOWELL NATIONAL HISTORICAL PARK QUARTER – MASSACHUSETTS

Released for Sale: February 4, 2019

Description: Lowell National Historical Park preserves and interprets the role of Lowell, MA, in the Industrial Revolution. The era was also defined in part by the "Mill Girls," young women recruited to work in the mills. They became an important voice for labor by advocating for better working conditions, supporting abolition, and embracing education. The reverse design depicts a mill girl working at a power loom. A view of Lowell, including the Boott Mill clock tower, is seen through the window.

AMERICAN MEMORIAL PARK QUARTER – NORTHERN MARIANA ISLANDS

Released for Sale: April 1, 2019

Description: American Memorial Park honors the thousands of American troops and residents of Saipan who gave their lives during the Marianas Campaign of World War II. At the Court of Honor, the American flag is displayed at the center of the Flag Circle and surrounded by the Navy, Marine Corps, Army, and Coast Guard flags. The reverse design depicts a young woman in traditional attire at the front of the Flag Circle and Court of Honor resting her hand on the plaque honoring the sacrifice of those who died in the Marianas Campaign.

WAR IN THE PACIFIC NATIONAL HISTORICAL PARK QUARTER – GUAM

Released for Sale: June 3, 2019

Description: The westernmost park of all the National Park Service sites, Guam's War in the Pacific National Historical Park honors the bravery, courage, and sacrifice of those participating in the campaigns of the Pacific Theater during World War II. The park also conserves and interprets a variety of amazing resources found on the Island of Guam. This reverse design depicts American forces coming ashore at Asan Bay.

SAN ANTONIO MISSIONS NATIONAL HISTORICAL PARK QUARTER – TEXAS

Released for Sale: August 26, 2019

Description: Established in the 1700s, the San Antonio Missions were among the largest concentrations of Spanish missions in North America and helped create the foundation for the city. The design depicts elements of the Spanish Colonial Real coin to pay tribute to the missions. Within the quadrants are symbols of the missions—wheat, arches and bell, a lion, and the San Antonio River.

AMERICAN INNOVATION™
$1 COIN PROGRAM

The American Innovation $1 Coin Act (Public Law 115-197) of 2018 authorized the minting and issuance of $1 coins emblematic of a significant innovation, innovator, or group of innovators representing each State, District of Columbia, Puerto Rico, Guam, American Samoa, U.S. Virgin Islands, and Northern Mariana Islands. Four new $1 coins with unique reverse designs will be released each year from 2019 through 2032 in the order the States ratified the U.S. Constitution or were admitted to the Union. After all State coins are released, those for the District of Columbia and territories will be issued. The common obverse of all coins in the series features a large, dramatic likeness of the Statue of Liberty.

2018 AMERICAN INNOVATION $1 INTRODUCTORY COIN

Released for Sale: December 14, 2018

Description: To introduce the new series in 2018, a special American Innovation $1 Coin was minted and issued. It has the same obverse as all the other coins in the series. The reverse design features a representation of President George Washington's signature on the first-ever U.S. patent issued on July 31, 1790. The U.S. Government granted the patent to Samuel Hopkins for "improvement in the making of pot ash and pearl ash." The stylized gears represent industry and innovation.

2019 AMERICAN INNOVATION $1 COIN – DELAWARE

Released for Sale: September 19, 2019

Description: Annie Jump Cannon was an internationally recognized astronomer who invented a system for classifying stars still used today. She combined two known models to create her own system based on the spectral characteristics of stars and personally classified more than 225,000. The reverse design features a silhouette of Cannon against the night sky, with a number of stars visible.

2019 AMERICAN EAGLE COIN PROGRAM

2019 AMERICAN EAGLE SILVER PROOF COIN

Released for Sale: January 10, 2019

Description: Each American Eagle Silver Proof contains one troy ounce of 99.9 percent pure silver. The obverse design is based on Adolph A. Weinman's 1916 "Walking Liberty" half dollar, widely considered one of the most beautiful American coins ever minted. It features Lady Liberty in full stride, enveloped in folds of the flag, with her right hand extended and branches of laurel and oak in her left. The reverse features a heraldic eagle with shield, an olive branch in the right talon and arrows in the left.

2019 PREAMBLE TO THE DECLARATION OF INDEPENDENCE PLATINUM PROOF COIN – "LIBERTY"

Released for Sale: January 31, 2019

Description: The obverse design of the 2019 Preamble to the Declaration of Independence Platinum Proof Coin portrays Lady Liberty keeping watch over prairies, lakes, and mountains as pioneers head westward. The wild terrain featured in the background evokes the quintessential American spirit to explore new territory and the freedom to pursue new landscapes, ideas, and ways of life. Her torch is an emblem of the guiding light that liberty provides, while the open book presents the rule of law and its equal application. The reverse design depicts an eagle in flight with an olive branch in its talons.

2019 AMERICAN EAGLE GOLD PROOF COIN

Released for Sale: March 7, 2019

Description: American Eagle Gold Proof Coins are manufactured in four sizes—one ounce, half-ounce, quarter-ounce, and one-tenth ounce. They are available individually or in a four-coin set. The obverse design features a rendition of Augustus Saint-Gaudens' full-length figure of Lady Liberty with flowing hair, holding a torch in her right hand and an olive branch in her left. The reverse features a male eagle carrying an olive branch flying above a nest containing a female eagle and her hatchlings.

2019 AMERICAN EAGLE PALLADIUM REVERSE PROOF COIN

Released for Sale: September 12, 2019

Description: Each coin contains one ounce of .9995 fine palladium. The obverse design features a high-relief likeness of "Winged Liberty" from the "Mercury Dime" obverse. The reverse design features a high-relief version of the 1907 American Institute of Architects Gold Medal reverse, which includes an eagle and a branch.

2019 AMERICAN BUFFALO GOLD COIN

Released for Sale: April 12, 2019

Description: The American Buffalo Gold Proof Coin is the first 24-karat gold proof coin ever struck by the U.S. Mint. Containing one ounce of .9999 fine gold, these lustrous coins are among the world's purest gold coins. They were authorized by Congress in 2005 and first minted in June 2006. They are struck at the United States Mint at West Point. The designs are based on the original 1913 Type I Buffalo nickel designed by James Earle Fraser. The obverse features a profile representation of a Native American, and the reverse features an American Buffalo.

2019 NATIVE AMERICAN $1 COIN

Released for Sale: February 13, 2019

Description: This year's reverse theme recognizes the contributions of American Indians to the U.S. space program. These culminated in the space walks of John Herrington (Chickasaw Nation) on the International Space Station in 2002. This and other pioneering achievements date back to the work of Mary Golda Ross (Cherokee Nation), considered the first Native American engineer in the space program. The reverse design features Ross writing calculations. In the background, an Atlas-Agena rocket launches into space, with an equation inscribed in its cloud. An astronaut conducts a spacewalk above. A group of stars in the field behind indicates outer space.

2019 COMMEMORATIVE COIN PROGRAMS

APOLLO 11 50TH ANNIVERSARY COMMEMORATIVE COINS

Released for Sale: January 24, 2019

Description: The Apollo 11 50th Anniversary Commemorative Coin Act (Public Law 114-182) authorized the minting and issuance of proof and uncirculated $5 gold, silver dollars (including a large proof five-ounce size), and clad half dollars in commemoration of the 50th anniversary of the first manned Moon landing on July 20, 1969. In accordance with the act, the Secretary of the Treasury approved the final designs, with the common obverse being selected through a juried competition. All coins issued through the program are curved. A special set featuring an Apollo 11 Proof Half Dollar and a Kennedy Half Dollar with an enhanced reverse proof finish was also issued through the program. The common obverse coin design features the inscriptions "MERCURY," "GEMINI," and "APOLLO" separated by phases of the Moon and a footprint on the lunar surface. The reverse is a representation of a close-up of the iconic "Buzz Aldrin on the Moon" photograph showing the visor and part of his helmet with a reflection showing astronaut Neil Armstrong, the American flag, and the lunar lander. Surcharges in the amount of $35 for each gold coin sold, $10 for each silver dollar sold, $5 for each clad half dollar sold, and $50 for each five-ounce proof silver dollar sold are authorized to be paid to the National Air and Space Museum's "Destination Moon" exhibit, Astronauts Memorial Foundation, and Astronaut Scholarship Fund.

AMERICAN LEGION 100TH ANNIVERSARY COMMEMORATIVE COINS

Released for Sale: March 14, 2019

Description: The American Legion 100th Anniversary Commemorative Coin Act (Public Law 115-65) authorizes the minting and issuance of proof and uncirculated $5 gold, silver dollars, and clad half dollars in recognition of the 100th anniversary of the American Legion. The Secretary of the Treasury approved the final designs. The American Legion 100th Anniversary Three-Coin Proof Set and Proof Silver Dollar and American Veterans Silver Medal Set were also issued through the program. The gold obverse design depicts the outer geometric rim from the American Legion emblem, the Eiffel Tower, and V for victory. The gold reverse depicts a soaring eagle and the American Legion emblem. The silver dollar obverse depicts the American Legion emblem adorned by oak leaves and a lily, while the reverse features the crossed American and American Legion flags with a fleur-de-lis and the inscription "100 YEARS OF SERVICE" above the flags. The clad half dollar obverse depicts two children standing and reciting the Pledge of Allegiance, beginning with the inscription "I PLEDGE ALLEGIANCE TO THE FLAG…" The half dollar reverse completes the phrase with the inscription "… OF THE UNITED STATES OF AMERICA." It depicts a waving American flag as seen from the children's point-of-view, with the American Legion emblem just above the flag. Surcharges in the amount of $35 for each gold coin sold, $10 for each silver dollar sold, and $5 for each clad coin sold are authorized to be paid to the American Legion for its programs to support veterans and members of the Armed Forces.

2019 PRESIDENTIAL SILVER MEDALS— JEFFERSON, MADISON, AND MONROE

Released for Sale: January 25 (Jefferson), May 6 (Madison), and August 8, 2019 (Monroe)

Description: These 99.9 silver medals—featuring the same designs as their familiar Presidential Bronze Medal counterparts—have a matte finish. The obverses of the Thomas Jefferson, James Madison, and James Monroe Presidential Silver Medals feature their traditional profiles. The reverses feature the inscription "PEACE AND FRIENDSHIP," symbolized by two clasped hands. Above the hands, the pipe of peace and tomahawk are crossed over each other. Presidential medals date back to the earliest days of the Republic and were often presented to American Indian chiefs and other leaders at events like treaty signings.

2018 Biennial Report to the Congress

as required by

The Coin Modernization, Oversight, and Continuity Act of 2010 (Public Law 111-302)

United States Mint

Department of the Treasury

April 2019

1. Background

The Coin Modernization, Oversight, and Continuity Act (CMOCA) of 2010, Public Law 111-302 (Act), authorizes the Secretary of the Treasury (Secretary) to conduct research and development (R&D) on alternative metallic materials for all circulating coins with the goal of reducing production costs. The Act also requires the Secretary to provide a biennial report to Congress on the status of coin production costs, cost trends for such production, and possible new metallic material or technologies for the production of circulating coinage.

The United States Mint (Mint), a bureau of the Department of the Treasury, submitted its first biennial report in December 2012, a second biennial report in December 2014, and a third for the year 2016, in June 2017. This report is the fourth biennial report produced as required by the Act.

2. Summary

The Mint manufactures new circulating coins, which supplement Federal Reserve Bank (FRB) coin inventories and meet the needs of commerce through the Nation's banking system. Typically, the Mint's annual production of new circulating coins is the net difference between total demand for circulating coins and total deposits received by the FRB from the banking system. The FRB buys new coins from the Mint at face value. The difference between the face value and the Mint's manufacturing cost is known as seigniorage. The Mint transfers seigniorage to the Treasury General Fund to help reduce the national debt.

3. Production Cost Comparison

Fiscal year (FY) 2018 unit costs are higher than those reported in our 2016 Biennial report. The unit costs for FY 2018 are: pennies (2.06 cents), nickels (7.53 cents), dimes (3.73 cents), and quarters (8.87 cents). The unit cost for both pennies and nickels remained above face value for the thirteenth consecutive fiscal year. While Federal Reserve orders for new coin decreased in FY 2017, orders decreased further in FY 2018. FY 2017 circulating coin shipments to the FRB decreased by 2.2 billion units (13.7 percent) to a total 14.1 billion coins compared to FY 2016. FY 2018 circulating coin shipments to the FRB of 13.7 billion units decreased by 400 million units (2.8 percent) compared to FY 2017.

UNIT COST OF PRODUCING AND DISTRIBUTING COINS BY DENOMINATION

2018	One-Cent	Five-Cent	Dime	Quarter-Dollar
Cost of Goods Sold	$0.0178	$0.0659	$0.0323	$0.0778
Selling, General & Administrative	$0.0025	$0.0085	$0.0045	$0.0099
Distribution to FRB	$0.0003	$0.0009	$0.0005	$0.0010
Total Unit cost	$0.0206	$0.0753	$0.0373	$0.0887

2017	One-Cent	Five-Cent	Dime	Quarter-Dollar
Cost of Goods Sold	$0.0156	$0.0564	$0.0284	$0.0711
Selling, General & Administrative	$0.0024	$0.0088	$0.0045	$0.0103
Distribution to FRB	$0.0002	$0.0008	$0.0004	$0.0010
Total Unit cost	$0.0182	$0.0660	$0.0333	$0.0824

2016	One-Cent	Five-Cent	Dime	Quarter-Dollar
Cost of Goods Sold	$0.0131	$0.0551	$0.0269	$0.0672
Selling, General & Administrative	$0.0017	$0.0071	$0.0034	$0.0080
Distribution to FRB	$0.0002	$0.0010	$0.0005	$0.0011
Total Unit cost	$0.0150	$0.0632	$0.0308	$0.0763

4. Research and Development

The Act authorizes the Secretary to conduct R&D on "possible new metallic materials or technologies for the production of circulating coins." The Act also specifies that before the second anniversary of its enactment, and biennially thereafter, the Secretary shall submit a report to Congress, analyzing production costs for each circulating coin, cost trends for such production, and possible new metallic materials or technologies for the production of circulating coins.

The Mint has performed diligent research for the last eight years to identify materials that satisfy the requirements of the Act, eliminating from consideration those that do not. As a result, the Mint has narrowed the wide field of elements and metallic alloys to several potential "seamless" alloys (meaning they would require no changes to coin-accepting equipment, but offer incremental savings), and a small number of potential "co-circulate" alternatives (meaning they would offer greater material savings, but coin-accepting equipment would require changes for the new coins to co-circulate with current coins) that would only see use in the 5-cent coin or in the 5-cent and dime coins.

In December 2012, the Mint delivered to the Congress the first (Phase I) biennial report in which it outlined six potential alloys to replace the current material. During the Phase II study, the Mint determined several of those materials not to be feasible for U.S. coinage. In December 2014, the Mint delivered the second (Phase II) biennial report, which detailed the results of

3

testing and evaluation of the initial alternatives and contained recommendations to further research a refined set of alternative materials. Phase III of the study involved more testing and evaluation to refine the identified alternatives along with research and development to identify other unique possibilities. This report provides an update on the Mint's study to identify and evaluate potentially seamless and co-circulate alternatives.

A. Alternative Materials

The materials that underwent more extensive evaluation during this period are:

- 80/20: A variation on the present cupronickel (75% copper (Cu)/25% nickel (Ni)), with more Cu, less Ni, and some manganese (Mn). Nominal composition of 77% Cu, 20% Ni, and 3% Mn.

- C99750T-M: A leaner potentially seamless alloy developed jointly with the National Institute of Standards and Technology (NIST), which contains less Cu and Ni and substitutes zinc (Zn) and Mn. Nominal composition 50.75% Cu, 14% Ni, 33% Zn, and 2.1% Mn. This alloy represents what we believe to be the leanest or lowest material cost possible. It also maintains the key seamless characteristics of electromagnetic signature (EMS) and color.

- Nickel Steel: A monolithic alloy developed by the Mint, which is austenitic (not attracted to magnets) and a less expensive co-circulate alternative to stainless steel. Nickel content is 25%, with the balance being lower cost iron and some manganese.

- Nickel Plated Silicon Steel: An alternative to the commonly used nickel or multi-ply plated steels in the world. This option could provide a co-circulate alternative with a distinguishable EMS and therefore more security than other commonly available plated steel coins.

A cost comparison table provided as attachment 1 estimates the material cost, total unit cost, and annual savings versus current coin compositions. The unit cost projections and resultant annual savings are very sensitive to fluctuations in metal cost and production volumes[1] so the estimates should be used as relative or directional and not budgetary.

With the prior research and the work accomplished this period, the following table summarizes the identified potential alternatives:

---

[1] Since a portion of the unit costs are distributed fixed production costs, overhead, and General & Administrative, changes in annual coin volumes can significantly affect the unit cost and projected savings.

Alternative	Seamless/Co-Circulate	Denominations	Testing Status
80/20	Potentially Seamless	5¢, 10¢, and 25¢	Full First Article qualifications complete with external validation by three coin acceptor manufacturers (CAMs).
C99750T-M	Potentially Seamless	5¢, 10¢, and 25¢	Small scale testing completed with samples validated by three external CAMs. Larger scale tests would be required to confirm production capable and confirm seamless.
Multi-ply Plated Steel (MPPS)	Co-Circulate	5¢ and 10¢	Large pre-production scale testing completed, would need First Article qualification.
Nickel Plated Steel (NPS)	Co-Circulate	5¢ and 10¢	Large pre-production scale testing completed, would need First Article qualification.
R52 Stainless (monolithic)	Co-Circulate	5¢ only	Small scale feasibility testing completed with limited external CAM testing.
Nickel Plated Silicon Steel	Co-Circulate	5¢ and 10¢	Small scale feasibility testing completed with limited external CAM testing.
Nickel Steel (monolithic)	Co-Circulate	5¢ only	Small scale feasibility testing completed with limited external CAM testing.

The first two materials in the above chart are potentially seamless materials, meaning that they are intended to work in current coin-accepting and handling equipment without modification. Extensive testing has been conducted on 80/20 monolithic 5-cent, and 80/20 clad 10-cent and 25-

cent denominations (half-dollar coins were not tested [2]) including comprehensive 1st Article qualification of both current strip suppliers and both circulating production facilities. In addition, the Mint conducted testing with three major CAMs to validate that the 80/20 is seamless with current U.S. cupronickel and cupronickel clad coins. The test used the CAMs' equipment. The C99750T-M material is potentially seamless for the 5-cent piece. It has the same EMS, dimensions, and piece weight as the current material. It is also a potentially seamless replacement for the cladding material of the dime, quarter-dollar, and half-dollar. Given that the major portion of clad coins is the copper core, the material savings from a change in the cladding composition are not significant. More development work is needed along with larger scale testing to establish C99750T-M as a viable seamless alternative; this is expected to take two years.

The remaining materials in the summary are co-circulate alternatives, meaning they do not have the same EMS, or piece weight, as that of the current U.S. coinage material. Co-circulate materials offer greater material savings, but would require modifications to coin-accepting and handling equipment.

The co-circulated materials listed—NPS, MPPS, and R52 Stainless—have been tested and evaluated, and details have been provided in earlier reports. The last two were alternatives developed by the Mint.

Nickel Steel is a lower cost alternative to stainless steel that was tested earlier. It is also austenitic (non-magnetic) with superior wear and corrosion resistance as compared to the current 5-cent. Its EMS and the monolithic construction mean it would be appropriate only for the 5-cent coin[3]. The Mint determined that Nickel Steel is viable for coining based on small scale testing. More extensive testing would be required to fully assess its coinability and production capability. It does not exhibit the mottled or orange peel appearance associated with the R52 stainless steel alternative tested earlier.

The Mint also developed another potentially unique co-circulate alternative – Nickel Plated Silicon Steel. The distinctive conductivity characteristics of silicon steel (also referred to as electrical steel), as compared to the low carbon steel used by other countries as a core material for plated coins, could provide a means of discriminating from the more commonly available nickel or multi-ply plated coins used by many countries. More extensive testing would be required to fully assess its viability.

---

[2] Testing for 80/20 was only completed on the dime and quarter-dollar, given the same clad construction the testing can readily be extrapolated to the half-dollar.

[3] If both denominations were made from the same monolithic material, the larger 5-cent could be counterfeited into the smaller but higher value 10-cent.

B. Production Improvements

The coin striking process is a whole system, no part of which can be changed without affecting another. These aspects include not only die shape and stamping force, but also level of detail, sharpness of transitions, and relief height in the coin's design; overall curvature of the coins' faces; and the upsetting process (which deforms the blank's material to the planchet's rim). The Mint considers these factors in optimizing the coin design.

During this current study, the Mint conceived an optimized system for the 5-cent coining process that can increase die life by modifying upset profiles and practices, as well as changing the geometry of the dies themselves together with subtle changes to the dies' designs that do not negatively affect the approved design or appearance. Specifically, matching planchet upset and die curvatures will reduce coining pressures around the coin edge, producing more uniform normal pressures. This "matched system" would enable coining presses to use less stamping force and still obtain optimal detail in the coins produced using current coinage materials. Less stamping force results in longer die life. Production testing has confirmed the effectiveness of this approach, and larger scale testing is currently in progress. Once completed, these refinements can be incorporated into the standard 5-cent design and testing undertaken to transition the approach to other denominations.

Matching planchet and die curvatures will also be beneficial when considering alternative materials, which in many cases are harder than current cupronickel. Greater hardness increases the coins' wear resistance, but the striking tonnage must be increased to get the same level of detail in the new coins as in the old ones. This greater striking pressure would reduce the die life and increase the stamping process cost. After the upset and die modifications, these harder new materials could be stamped to get the same image detail with the same tonnage as current production.

The Mint saw promising results when the "matched system" was used on the current coinage material, alternative materials, and also with pushback-blanked material (as opposed to conventional blanked material). Beyond that, the optimization also shows great promise with other circulating denominations, whether alternative materials or current materials are used. The Mint contracted with an independent company to perform a study on the formation of the coins' rims in the optimized design. The contractor used a prototype upsetting tool and tested several different profiles and methods of upsetting blanks and determined that a tapered upset with a concave facing formed the best rims of coins, and that tapered upset with a convex facing was nearly as good. Continued testing and evaluation are in progress. Push Back Blanking (PBB) is a blanking process which cuts blanks from coils of material annealed by an external supplier versus the current process of cutting the blanks from the cold rolled coil first (the harder cold-rolled strip facilitates blanking with our conventional blanking process, a special blanking die is necessary for the "softer" annealed strip) and then annealing the blanks internally.

C. Findings and Conclusions

The Mint tested and evaluated both seamless and co-circulate during this period, resulting in the development of two unique co-circulate alternatives. In addition, the Mint continued to develop and evaluate of several concepts to improve the production of circulating coin.

a) Seamless Materials

1. After extensive testing, the Mint determined 80/20 to be a potentially seamless alternative for producing 5-cent (monolithic), 10-cent, and 25-cent (when bonded to a copper core) circulating coins that matches the current materials' key characteristics of EMS, color, and piece weight. The Mint completed qualification of the strip suppliers and the Mint production processes and three major CAMS completed external validation.

2. The Mint tested C99750T-M, a potentially seamless alternative developed by the Mint, on a small scale internally with CAM validation externally. It shows promise of being able to further reduce the material costs while still being able to work in current coin-accepting and -handling equipment without modification. The Mint recommends larger scale testing and development to determine if C99750T-M is a viable seamless alternative.

b) Co-Circulate Materials

1. The Mint developed two unique co-circulate alternatives, Nickel Steel and Nickel Plated Silicon Steel, and completed initial testing to confirm coinability and coin recognition/sorter signature. The Mint recommends larger scale tests to fully evaluate them as viable co-circulate alternatives.

c) Production Improvement

1. Tests involving changing the geometry of the 5-cent dies, together with subtle changes to the dies' designs that do not negatively affect the approved design or appearance, have shown improved die life in production trials. The Mint recommends continued testing with migration to other denominations and incorporation into future designs.

2. The Mint completed structured trials with various rimming profiles on the 5-cent coin. The results show promise and can yield incremental efficiencies in the production of circulating coin and other Mint products, so development work should continue. The Mint recommends small-scale coining trials continue followed by production-scale die life testing. Objective data gathered during these coining trials will be used to develop a

Finite Element Analysis (FEA) model to reduce the need for as many trials in the future and enable the application of the optimization to other Mint products.

Lightning Source UK Ltd.
Milton Keynes UK
UKHW05082801 0620
364110UK00007B/360